INDIA'S PLACE IN THE WORLD

A History And Analysis Of International Organizations

&

India's Growing Role On The World Stage

KRISHNA CHILUKURI

LEAD▶START
Publishing
empowering thought

978-93-81115-73-2

Cover   Mishta Roy
Layouts   Ajay Shah, Mumbai
Printing   Repro India Ltd, Navi Mumbai

Published in India 2011 by
LEADSTART PUBLISHING PVT LTD
Trade Centre, Level 1, Bandra Kurla Complex
Bandra (E), Mumbai 400 051, INDIA
T + 91 22 40700804   **F** +91 22 40700800
E info@leadstartcorp.com **W** www.leadstartcorp.com

US Office
Axis Corp
7845 E Oakbrook Circle
Madison, WI 53717, USA

Disclaimer The views expressed in this book are those of the Author and do not purport to be those of the Publisher.

To My Parents
Mrunalini & Hanumantha Rao
Chilukuri

ABOUT THE AUTHOR

KRISHNA CHILUKURI is a 'Dean's Merit List' graduate of the Indian School of Business, Hyderabad. He also completed a certification in Advanced Studies at Thunderbird School of Global Management, Phoenix, Arizona. Krishna Chilukuri has over 15 years experience in the corporate world, working in different countries around the world, including over a decade in the United States.

His interests include Geopolitics, Strategy and the Environment.

He can be reached at: krishna2010@global.t-bird.edu

Contents

PREFACE

WHY THIS BOOK?

India's growth in recent years has attracted a number of predictions about India (and China), as the next super powers and the shift of global power to Asia and the East. In my research on the topic, I have come across books that broadly fall into one of two categories. One group of authors go hundreds of years back in time, when India and China were dominant civilizations, and these books proclaim that the time has come for these ancient civilizations to rightfully take their place in the 21st century. The other set of authors travel fifty to a hundred years into the future, extrapolating the economies of India and China at current growth rates, to show how dominant they will be and how the balance will shift to the East. While both these factors and analysis have their merits, I believe it is more important to understand the current structure of the world and the events of the last fifty or sixty years; India's place in this structure, and how and what India needs to do to chart the course of her future.

We live in a complex world with a multitude of competing sovereign nations – countries with varying economic, political and military power. International Organizations such as the UN, IMF and the WTO, have been set up to bring some structure to the interactions between these nations and to provide a framework to solve global issues and crises. These organizations can wield tremendous power and countries that have a major influence in them can and do take advantage of their power for their own benefit or to promote their own agenda.

The current structure of the world was established after the Second World War, led by the US and its Western Allies who have given themselves control over the decision- making process in key bodies, thereby wielding tremendous influence in world events. But in recent years, developing countries led by India and China, are pushing for reforms that will lessen the stranglehold of the US and its allies and give a bigger voice to them, as a way to balance the power structure.

The most significant restructuring of the world was spearheaded by the United States when the US State Department, in 1939, began working on a new international organization to replace the failed League of Nations. US President, Franklin Roosevelt, coined the term 'the United Nations', which was formally launched in 1945. The restructuring of the world's economic and financial system was undertaken at the Bretton Woods Conference in 1944, led again by the US. At this conference, two of the three pillars on which the world financial and economic systems now stand, namely the IMF (International Monetary Fund) the WB (The World Bank group), were founded. The third pillar, GATT (General Agreement on Trade and Tariff), which later morphed into the WTO (World Trade Organization), came out of negotiations initiated under the UN for a new organization called the ITO (International Trade Organization). As the most powerful nations among the founding members of the IMF, WB and the UN Security Council, the US and its allies in the developed world, have maintained their dominance and influence in world events. But the dominant status of the United States is under threat (the US has already lost its hegemonic status in the strict definition of the term), and the institutions that were created more than fifty years ago, are beginning to lose their significance in some circumstances and are redefining their purpose and structure in others.

The economies in the US and in many Western nations in Europe, are going through a prolonged crisis, putting enormous strain on their ability to use their financial-market clout to influence world events. In contrast, the economies of India and China continue to grow rapidly, enhancing their economic wealth and consequently their power. In order to have a bigger influence in world events, India and China must work towards a new world order. To have a bigger say in the decisions that affect the world, they must play an active role in the restructuring of these international institutions. This is far from easy.

A peaceful, orderly restructuring of the Institutions and their objectives, as well as their governance and the rebalance of world power, should be the strategic goal of India's foreign policy. It is my attempt in this book to collate and analyze the current structure of the world as well as the major events of the past sixty years. I have focused on: the United Nations as a global institution; the UN Security Council and collective security; international monetary and financial structure through the IMF and the World Bank; trade and commerce through GATT and WTO; and finally the impact of global warming and the international response to it. I will also attempt to indicate possible directions and options India could take to exert more influence and power in the world through these institutions.

While the nature of the topic is technical, I have tried to make it as readable for everyone as possible. I hope this book will help students and citizens of India understand the nature of today's world and engage in debate as well as put pressure on policy makers to take an active role in shaping India's role in the world.

Finally, a suggestion to my readers – in the good old days we were advised to read a book with a dictionary by our side. Today, I recommend readers refer to the internet, Wikipedia.org, websites of global institutions, as well as Google the vast amount of information accumulated on the internet, to gain a more in-depth understanding of their world and the topics touched upon in this book.

An Introduction

1

India's economy has grown tremendously in the last decade, benefitting from the liberalization policies it adopted in the aftermath of the balance of payments crisis in 1991. Luckily for India, the liberalization policies came at the right time. It allowed the country to benefit from the wave of globalization that has swept the global economy in the recent decade. India's GDP (Gross Domestic Product), grew from US$ 460 Billion in 2000, to more than US$ 1.2 Trillion by 2008, and is projected to end the year 2010 with an economy the size of 1.5 Trillion USD[1]. This is a tripling of the economy in the last decade, when the economy has grown at an average of over 7% compared to India's pre-liberalization growth rates of 2-3%. The per capita income and consequently the purchasing power have also grown over the last decade from US $450 per person to over US $1200 by the end of 2008. This has led to better standards of living and optimism in the country.

---

1 World Bank country report: India www.worldbank.org

INDIA			
(Source World Bank Report)			
	2000	2005	2007	2008
Economy				
GDP (current US$) (billions)	460.18	810.15	1,176.89	1,217.49
GDP growth (annual %)	4.0	9.4	9.1	7.1
Inflation, GDP deflator (annual %)	3.5	4.1	4.9	7.3
Agriculture, value added (% of GDP)	23	19	18	18
Industry, value added (% of GDP)	26	29	30	29
Services, etc., value added (% of GDP)	50	52	52	53
Exports of goods and services (% of GDP)	13	20	21	24
Imports of goods and services (% of GDP)	14	23	25	30

Source: The World Bank group

This tremendous growth of the economy has also helped India make substantial progress towards the targets of its Millennium Development goals, including reduction of poverty. While there are debates about the extent of poverty reduction, there can be no doubt that the incidence of poverty has come down in the past decade. According to data released by the Statistical Institute of India using the criterion defined by the Planning Commission for the definition of poverty, the poverty rate in India has come down from being more than 50% of the population in the 1970s to less than 28% in 2005[2] and while data for 2010 is not yet available most experts expect the rate to fall further despite the global economic slowdown in 2008-2009.

Other social indicators have also shown great improvements. Life expectancy has increased from 62 at the beginning of the decade in 2000, to an estimated 70 years by the end of 2009. Child mortality, which is the incidence of death among children less than 5 years of age and is measured in deaths per 1000 children, has also fallen from 91 in 2000 to 72 in 2007. The number continues to fall, according to the World Bank report which tracks the progress towards the Millennium goals[3]. Many experts have opined that the only way for the world to achieve the first target of the Millennium goals will be through the continuing growth of India and China, where a substantial percentage of the world's disadvantaged people live and have benefitted from the growth of their respective economies.

India has made great strides over the last decade. However, there is no doubt it has a long way to go to reduce poverty, increase life expectancy and eliminate poverty. Lifting the quality of life and social equality, are also issues of importance. These goals require a combination of the right economic policies along with policies that promote freedom, a right to education and health, equality and other social goals. The discussion of these economic and social policies is a considerable task but it is not the focus of this book. For the purposes of this book, I am going to assume that India will continue to grow at rates greater than 7-8% every year, meet most or all the Millennium

---

2 http://www.planningcommission.gov.in/news/prmar07.pdf
3 http://www.worldbank.org.in

Development goals in the coming 2-4 decades and become a large, economic power in terms of the size of the country's GDP, over the next few decades. This is quite possible as has been demonstrated by China, which started its new economic journey after the process of liberalization was initiated by Deng Xiaoping in 1978.

China has grown to become the second largest economy in the world and the incidence of poverty has come down from over 50% in 1983 to less than 8% in 2001[4]. China has huge foreign exchange reserves in excess of 2 Trillion USD and a growing presence and influence on the world. China's presence can be specially noticed in Africa, where it has sometimes become an alternative to IMF and WB loans. In my opinion though, China has not done enough to assert itself on the world stage nor taken concrete steps to restructure the nature of International Institutions and China's role in them. China does not have a voice on the world stage that is commensurate with its power. It plays relatively insignificant roles at the IMF and the World Bank, where its voting rights are not in line with the size of its economy. While China does have a seat as a permanent member of the Security Council at the UN, it has not been able to influence many of the decisions made there, nor has it shown any leadership in helping to solve global humanitarian or security crises. The US and its allies continue to make the majority of decisions at the Security Council, including resolutions to invade Iraq and Libya, despite China's vocal opposition to these resolutions. The US also provokes China by supplying arms to Taiwan – which China has been unable to address through the Security Council despite its permanent membership.

---

4 http://go.worldbank.org/QXOQI9MP30

China does not influence many of the important decisions that are made in the realm of international finance or international trade despite being the world's factory. As the second largest economy in the world, it should exert a greater influence on decisions made at the IMF and the WTO. Let us be sure that China does have a huge and fast growing economy, a large and rapidly modernizing military and a growing influence on the world stage – but we can argue that it has not yet mastered the art of wielding this power nor has it asserted itself on the global agenda. This is a predicament that India can easily find itself in within the next two decades.

With an economy that can triple every decade, India's GDP could reach 4.5 Trillion USD by 2020 and to more than 13 Trillion by 2030 – the size of the US GDP today. This growing economic status will propel India into the forefront of global politics and leadership, but will India be ready, willing and capable of shouldering the leadership role? The answer rests solely on the ambitions India harbors, the strategies and policies she implements. The time is now for India strategists and thinkers to help shape India's foreign policy to formulate a strategy for accumulating and wielding State Power in the coming decades.

STATE POWER

Much as we might like to romanticize the world as one happy human family, it is made up of sovereign nations which are in a constant power struggle with each other to control resources, impose their will and wield power for the betterment of their citizens. Through the centuries, different countries have used their hard and soft power to colonize, impose their system of government, their style of business and institutional structures on others in order to accumulate wealth, resources and for the overall benefit their citizens. Dominant powers such as the UK in the 17th and 18th centuries, and the US, after the Second World War, have acted as hegemons to protect and further their national interests. The single most important concern for a country or nation is to perpetuate itself. The constitution of any country calls for its citizens to protect and strengthen their nation. A world made up of such sovereign countries, whose primary objective is self-preservation and growth, is inherently competitive in nature. Countries accumulate and display their power in three main realms – economic, cultural and military.

These ideas are borrowed from the international relations theory called political realism. While there are a number of other theories of international relations, I believe growing powers such as India, must review their policies through the lens of political realism. The destabilizing forces in the world order created by rising middle powers such as India and China, will create distortions in the balance of power between nations. The response by the current super powers to this emergence, will be to revert back to political realism as their politicians and citizens perceive threats to their national interests. The strategic goal of rising powers should be to establish a new balance of power and a new global order. To be able to influence and change the current global order they have to accumulate State power. They have to be active participants in global institutions and use their State Power appropriately and responsibly.

State Power is the capacity of a country to influence and direct the decisions and actions of other countries in order to protect and further its national interests. States also acquire power (economic, cultural and military), to build national well-being, preserve domestic peace and tranquility and ensure freedom from coercion by other countries. The core of any nation's policies and actions is built to protect and enhance the nation's vital and strategic interests. Vital interests for a country include its sovereignty, secure borders, the well-being of its citizens and domestic tranquility. Strategic interests include access to resources essential for national power, immunity from intimidation, both internal and external, and securing of strategic advantages to further national power. State power is built on a country's size, population, economic and military strength; cultural distinction and vitality. It is also a function of how other countries perceive and believe a nation to possess these resources and advantages and its willingness to use them to enforce its will.

Cultural vitality and distinction is the ability of a country to inspire other countries to emulate its ideas, admire its achievements, and use its institutional systems and language. Countries often project their culture abroad through the arts, intellectual ideology, moral themes and lifestyles. This enhances the prestige of a country and raises the acceptance by other countries to receiving proposals from it – adding emotional appeal to the country's political, economic and military strengths and endeavors.

The economic strength of a country is measured in terms of the country's financial assets, size of its GDP (Gross Domestic Product), the per capita income of its citizens, the human development index, which measures the quality of life, and its participation in world economy and trade, as well as investment flows. Economic strength is built through international trade and investments, which are powerful tools that can be used to help or hurt other nations. Powerful nations such as the US, often use economic sanctions as a coercive tool to influence the behavior of adversaries and change their policies to benefit America and American companies, sometimes to the detriment of local companies and people.

Military strength is the most visible element of a country's power. It provides an immediate and brutal means for a nation to impose its will on other countries. A country can build a strong military if they have the ability to equip, train and maintain the different branches. Today, the military depends heavily on technological superiority for both their weaponry and communication systems. The ability for strategic planning and execution also builds a nation's strength. The military power of any country, despite its size and weaponry, is only as strong as the nation's readiness and willingness to use it to further its interests.

Building, managing and wielding State Power requires significant strategic and diplomatic capabilities but it is fundamentally built on economic power. In the history of the world, no state or country has been powerful on the world stage without being an economic powerhouse. Protecting and enhancing economic wellbeing and growth is a key strategic component of any government's policy. Hegemons and dominant powers make the most of their strategic choices and treaties to enhance their economic power. Realists will be quick to point out the advantages for the US that are built into the current structure of the world.

With an economy that is growing at more than 8%, leading to rising economic and financial capabilities, India must begin a comprehensive strategy of accumulating state power and well defined guidelines that direct the use of this State Power.

Hᴇɢᴇᴍᴏɴɪᴄ Sᴛᴀʙɪʟɪᴛʏ Tʜᴇᴏʀʏ & ᴛʜᴇ Wᴀsʜɪɴɢᴛᴏɴ Cᴏɴsᴇɴsᴜs

It is important to be aware of a few theoretical models of global political economy as well as international relations theory, before we can begin to understand the nature of today's world and India's place in it. The three classical theories of global political economy are Liberalism, Economic Nationalism or Mercantilism and Structuralism.

Liberals believe in free markets and the ability of free markets to create prosperity for all those who engage in it. They are opposed to government intervention (or a minimum of government intervention), in the market and advocate open borders, free flows of capital and in the power of markets. They believe open markets are best suited to set prices, balance demand and supply and optimize investments. They also believe in individual rights and freedoms as essential for a society to have free markets. The central principle of Liberalism is that when all individuals focus on their own profits, the entire economy benefits and grows.

Adam Smith was the first thinker and economist who fully described this principle in his books, *The Theory of Moral Sentiments* and *The Wealth of Nations*. Smith believed that when an individual pursues his self-interest, he indirectly promotes the good of society, 'by pursuing his own interest, he frequently promoted that of the society more effectually than when he intended to promote it'[5].

---

5 http://www.unc.edu/depts/econ/byrns_web/EC434/HET/Pioneers/smith.htm

Smith also introduced the famous metaphor of the 'invisible hand' of the market. The invisible hand is a result of market forces that include self-interest, competition, supply and demand which are capable of allocating scare resources in the economy in the most efficient manner.

Another key underpinning of this philosophy is the theory of comparative advantage proposed by David Ricardo[6]. This theory states that if all nations were to produce goods in which they had a comparative advantage (lowest opportunity cost compared with other nations) and trade amongst themselves, then everyone would benefit.

A variant of liberalism is embedded liberalism, where the need for state intervention in times of crises is recognized and warranted. The most powerful countries today are based on the liberal view either extreme or embedded. Extreme liberals believe that governments should play no role in directing the economy, while embedded liberals believe in limited government intervention to correct market failures and imbalances. The US is the strongest advocate of liberalism and its free markets have dominated the global economy since the end of the Second World War. International Institutions such as the IMF and the WB also have their underpinnings based on this ideology. Globalization and the rise of multinationals in recent years is the direct outcome of Liberalism promoted by the US and the International Institutes it controls.

The idea of economic nationalism is based on strategies countries employ to protect domestic industries

---

6 According to the WTO website – This is arguably the single most powerful insight into economics http://www.wto.org/english/thewto_e/whatis_e/tif_e/fact3_e.htm

and gain an advantage over others as they compete for resources to build their nation's power. The government plays a highly interventionist role, creating barriers for companies from other countries while employing strategies and policies that benefit domestic companies. A number of growing or emerging economies like China, tend to adopt economic nationalism. By keeping its currency artificially undervalued so it can continue to export its goods while making imports expensive, China has systematically built its foreign reserves and grown its economy. It is common for countries which implement economic nationalist policies to provide protection to domestic industries by imposing high import tariffs, subsidizing local industries and preventing or controlling 100% foreign direct investment in certain sectors and industries in its economy. South Korea encouraged and provided financial and policy support to large family-owned organizations called Chaebols, as a way to develop local industry.

India has a number of policies based on this idea such as requiring domestic content for foreign manufacturers that set up plants in India, imposing tariffs on imports and limiting FDI in the retail or insurance industries. It is interesting to note that one of the most famous of the proponents of economic nationalism was Alexander Hamilton (who wrote the Constitution of the US), who in his report to the first US Congress, proposed trade protection and a strong role for the government in promoting domestic industries to protect America from Britain – the most powerful nation at that time.

Structuralism is a theory of political economy that is based on the views of Marx and Lenin, but no longer has any relation to Communism or Soviet-style economic planning. Structuralism is based on the idea of class conflict between those who have capital and those who do not. It has also been used to explain the conflict of interest between dominant powers and their relationship with other emerging and weaker powers. It is a useful theory to analyze and counter argue the actions taken by those with liberal or economic nationalist ideologies, specifically for growing economies. Lenin postulated the law of capitalist imperialism where capitalist countries with accumulated capital, are compelled to seize colonies which serve as markets, investment outlets and sources of food and raw materials. A later variation of Structuralism, also known as the Dependence Theory, postulated that the global economy and powerful nations enslave less developed countries by making them dependant on them for capital and access to global markets. The major exports for these less developed countries are raw materials and other commodities with declining terms of trade (they receive a lower value for their exports every year), which enslaves them to export more and more each year. This idea is also known as 'the development of underdevelopment[7]'. The view of Intellectual Hegemony has also risen from the Structuralist perspective which postulates that powerful countries promulgate an ideology that supports and legitimizes its interests and allows them to exploit other nations.

The Hegemonic Stability theory is an outgrowth of economic nationalism but one which uses embedded liberal ideas to achieve its end. Hegemony is the dominance of one

---

7 The argument goes that if developing and underdeveloped countries continue to focus on their comparative advantage which essentially is agriculture, mining and other commodity exports they will remain underdeveloped and dependant on the markets in the developed countries forever. Comparative advantage maintains and even promotes the development of underdevelopment in poor countries.

country or an alliance of countries, over others. Hegemonic Stability theory is used to explain how international markets work best when a hegemon (the dominant power), creates a stable market by underwriting the costs of such a market, but in return, benefits from this open international market. A hegemon provides military and security protection to its allies and opens its market to international trade but in turn requires participants to open their markets for the products and services of the hegemon. The hegemon also provides monetary stability and capital investments and acts as the lender of last resort. By creating a stable and open international market, the hegemon benefits by being able to export its goods, import raw materials and food at low costs and have new avenues for capital investment. At the height of their power, hegemons are so economically and militarily dominant, that they have no hesitation in opening up their markets. They also demand access to the markets of others and benefit from their technological and production superiority.

Proponents of the Hegemonic Stability theory recognize three hegemonic stability eras in modern history[8]: the 17th century, when Holland was the hegemon; the 18th and 19th centuries when Great Britain was the hegemon; and the post-world war II era with the United States as the hegemon. After the Second World War, the US provided many of its allies with military protection through NATO and other treaties, opened its market, provided them with capital, pegged the dollar to gold, made it the currency of international trade, creating monetary and economic stability up till the mid-70s.

---

8 David Balaam, Michael Veseth, *Introduction to International Political Economy*, 4th edition, Pearson Prentice Hall, 2008

The Great Depression of 1929, which started with the stock market crash of 29 October 1929, also known as Black Tuesday, was the longest most widespread and the deepest depression of the 20th century. The depression devastated many economies and imposed widespread poverty. This was also a period when there was no hegemon to stabilize the world economy. Great Britain was still too weak from the end of the First World War and the US was not ready to take on the mantle of a hegemon to provide the stability needed for the global economy to recover and prosper.

The first response of most countries to the depression was to invoke economic nationalist policies such as the infamous Smoot-Hawley Tariff Act of 1930[9]. Other responded with similar retaliatory tariffs which exacerbated the collapse of the global economy. The Smoot-Hawley Tariff Act in America, raised import tariffs on over 20,000 imported goods to record levels. The ensuing retaliatory tariffs enacted by its partners, reduced American imports and exports by more than 50%. The US also tightened its credit policy by increasing interest rates and devalued its currency in an effort to gain a competitive advantage for its exports.

Many economists argue that US protectionist policies made the depression of 1929 into the Great Depression and prolonged it. The lessons learnt from the effects of these policies led to the dominance of the embedded liberal views held by the world's economic powers. The start of a new world economic structure was created at the Bretton Woods Conference, where the IMF, WB and GATT, were embedded into the world monetary and economic system.

---

9 http://future.state.gov/when/timeline/1921_timeline/smoot_tariff.html

One of the most influential economists of the 20th century, John Maynard Keynes, proposed his version of liberalism known as the Keynesian Theory of Economics or the Embedded Liberal View. Keynes proposed that the State should have a role in steadying the 'invisible hand' of the market. He believed that positive government action was both useful and necessary to deal with problems that the invisible hand could not set right, such as a depression and monopolies. He proposed increased state intervention and spending during the Great Depression as a way to stabilize and grow the economy. His embedded liberal views formed the basis of the founding of international institutions such as the IMF and the WB, that have provided stability and governed global trade and economy since their founding in 1944. The Bretton Woods system established rules for commercial and financial relations among the world's major countries and governance of these relations.

This was also the beginning of the third era of hegemonic stability. The US was the most dominant power in the capitalist world at the end of the Second World War, with an economy that was more than half the global economy. Having learnt the negative effects of tariffs on its economy and the prolonging of the depression in part due to the Smoot-Hawley act, the US wanted to ensure this did not happen again. The US took on the role of the hegemon, providing security to Europe, opening its markets, lowering tariff rates, making the dollar the global currency and pegging it to gold, acting as a lender of last resort, sometimes directly and sometimes through the IMF and WB. The US also demanded that Europe and other countries open their markets to American goods and services to usher in the third hegemonic stability era.

The Washington Consensus is a synonym for market fundamentalism and was coined by John Williamson, to describe the policies that the US Treasury Department, through the Bretton Woods institutions of the IMF and WB, prescribed to developing and underdeveloped economies. This included a set of specific economic policy prescriptions such as opening up of a country's economy through liberalization, increasing interest rates, opening up to foreign investment and capital etc. It is no surprise that this specific set of policies are also recommended by the IMF and are also referred to as the IMF conditionality. This term is also associated with neoliberal policies and is seen as an attempt by the US to propagate its ideology and influence the actions (wielding its power), of other countries, overriding their national sovereignty concerns. The IMF imposed these conditions when providing loans to weak economies that faced a balance of payment crisis. But the results of these actions are mixed. The IMF has been most criticized for its role in the Asian financial crisis and has since promised to drop the 'one solution fits all' prescription.

Though the US is no longer a hegemon, it is still a powerful and dominant country in the world. But it is slowly seeing its power diminish. This is going to have an effect on the stability of international relations as well as herald the beginnings and creation of a new world order. The recent economic recession of 2008-2009, has exposed a number of fault lines in the ability of the US to continue to be the world's economic engine. The debacle in Iraq has undermined its status as the most dominant power in the world.

The quick turnarounds for the economies of China and India indicate the rise of a new economic world order. Will the US continue to advocate free markets if it begins to see that it cannot compete in them anymore? To understand how these economic changes and shifts in national power are going to affect the global order, we need to also understand two important theories of international relations: the Balance of Power and Power Transition.

THEORIES OF INTERNATIONAL RELATIONS

The Power Transition theory was postulated by A.F.K. Organski, in his book titled *World Politics*[10], and can be viewed as an extension of the Hegemonic Stability theory of political economics. According to the Power Transition theory, the likelihood of war increases when a rising power is dissatisfied with the current state of the world as defined by the hegemon and rises to challenge the hegemon. The outcome of the war establishes a new hegemon and a new period of stability as defined by the new hegemon. The current hegemon tries to prevent and block the new rising powers by establishing alliances and by using its soft and hard State power to block access to resources, markets and technology. Organski also believes that peace is best preserved when there is an imbalance of power between nations. Organski divided nations into Great Powers, Middle Powers and Small Powers.

The Great Powers include the hegemon, as well as potential rivals to the dominant state. The Middle Powers have regional significance similar to the dominant state but are not big or strong enough to challenge the hegemon. Small Powers make up the rest of the countries that are under a regional or global hegemon. As with the Hegemonic Stability theory, the Power Transition theory also postulates that the dominant or Great Powers create a set of political

---

10 A.F.K. Organski, *World Politics*, Alfred A. Knopf Publishing, 1968

and economic structures and rules that create a stable global system and at the same time benefit the Great Power the most.

Much of the history of wars between nations can be viewed through this theory. As discussed before, historians define three periods of hegemonic stability eras defined by the dominant powers of the time – the Dutch in the 17th century (wrested from Spain in a series of power struggles and battles in the 1600s); the British in the 18th and 19th centuries; and the US, post the Second World War. Eugene Wittkopf has explored past wars in the context of the Power Transition theory in his book, *World Politics: Trend and Transformation,* and has explained much of past conflict through the lens of the Power Transition theory.

Basing India's strategy on this theory would mean that India would need to grow its economy large enough, build its military strong enough, and spread its culture and soft power far enough, to challenge the US and other rising Middle Powers such as China. A change in the world order would be possible by challenging US hegemony. But with many emerging giants such as China, Brazil and Russia, a change in hegemon in the 21st century could mean a complicated and very destructive war. There is no clear single challenger to the current hegemon which is slowly losing its relative power advantage over rising powers. The future strategy may require a different basis, a different theory and approach to managing global relations and power position for India. A future shift in global power most likely will not be defined by the outcome of a global war as has happened in the past but rather, by a change in the structure of world organizations, institutions and governing bodies. New alliances and trade relationships will herald changes in the global economy. The need to tackle problems that affect all humanity such as global warming, will bring new co-operation among nations.

The 21st century is a vastly different era in human history. Technology, globalization and trade have integrated nations into the world system like never before. Never before have nations become so connected and so dependent on other nations, with weaponry power so deadly that they can wipe out humanity from the face of the earth. These conditions lay the ground for a different view of the power structure of the world and how it will shift in the future. We cannot sustain another global war for power transition and a new hegemon – hence we must look for alternative solutions to power transition.

The Balance of Power theory is the exact opposite of the Power Transition theory. Nations that adopt a strategy based on the Balance of Power theory, strive to define and set regional and global rules and treaties that prevent any one nation from enforcing its will upon the rest. By forming alliances and organizations that allow the creation of platforms, international law members strive to reach a just equilibrium. When there are multiple countries and states that are equal in State Power, they can either engage in a hegemonic war to determine who will be the dominant power or they can co-operate and create a balance or power environment. The central strategy adopted by countries based on this principle is for self-preservation. States try to avoid the dominance of one state by allying themselves with other states until equilibrium is reached. The cold war can be viewed through this theory where there were two competing super powers and most countries chose one side or the other to create a balance of power, which prevented a large world war.

Equilibrium of international State Power is the basis for the formation of international law. Under a hegemonic system, the dominant power sets out international law that is in its best interests but when a Balance of Power system takes over, the stage is set for the creation of a more just international system and law. There are competing powers of equal strength to enforce international law when one of them ignores the law or acts solely according to its convenience and interests. A true Balance of Power system could be the ultimate triumph of the human civilization whereby the nations of the world are bound to each other in a just system of international law and prosperity reigns. It seems that we are headed in that direction.

There are a number of growing powers in the world including the BRIC countries, the European Union, and possibly the formation of the African Union, in the next decade or two. The world is more inter-connected than ever before and advances in transportation and communication have connected people around the world. The US is no longer a dominant hegemon and the rising powers of today do not harbor intentions of being the next hegemon. All these presage the golden age of the 21st century's world equilibrium. There will no doubt be conflicts of interest and the occasional violation of international laws, but nations and states around the world will be more tightly bound by trade and commerce, travel and connectedness.

The major challenges to humanity in the coming decades will not be hegemonic wars but common problems affecting all nations, such as global warming, climate change, terrorism and poverty. As countries get more inter-connected and economies are linked like never before, maintaining the economic and social growth needed to sustain prosperity and lift billions out of poverty and poor living conditions, will become the major policy challenges of the 21st century.

Basing India's strategy on the Balance of Power theory would mean India would have to grow its presence and influence in global bodies such as the UN and the WTO, and be an active participant in the creation of international law and treaties that are going to govern all future relations and activity between nations. India must proactively engage with the world. Integration with the world system, which includes trade, security and wellbeing, is the key and her economic and foreign policy decisions must reflect this direction. We must have a good understanding of the current world architecture which includes international organizations such as the UN, IMF, WB, WTO etc and how India can influence policy and international law that is being drafted at these institutions.

THE CURRENT STATE OF THE WORLD

The end of the Second World War witnessed the emergence of the US as the dominant or hegemonic power in the capitalist world[11]. The UK, which was the dominant power till the First World War, was no longer the hegemon, but worked with the US to create international institutions such as the IMF, the WB and the trade treaty referred to as GATT (General Agreement on Trade and Tariff), which embodied the Embedded Liberal perspective of the world. Through

---

11 At the world level there was a 'balance of power' relationship of tension between the Capitalist countries and the Communist countries. Within the group of Capitalist countries, the US acted as a Hegemon and provided collective security through treaties like NATO as well as financial stability through the IMF and the WB.

these institutions and treaties the US and its allies promoted their view of the world.

Capital in the US needed new investment avenues. Multi-national companies based in the US and Western Europe needed new markets to sell their wares as their domestic markets were getting saturated. Through instruments such as Structural Adjustment Programs, the US forced countries to adopt a more liberal economic system that pried open their markets. This allowed the more sophisticated multi-national companies to capture global market share before companies in developing countries had the time and opportunity to develop their abilities to compete. The US, using its domestic and foreign policy strategy in combination with the IMF Structural Lending programs and the WTO, pushed countries to liberalize and open their markets – sometimes faster than the societies in these countries could adapt to.

The rapid social and economic changes brought about by these forced liberalizations caused chaos, social upheaval and suffering. The Asian financial crisis is one such example where the IMF exacerbated the crisis and caused social chaos in South Korea, Malaysia and Thailand. A number of scholars have written about the policies and criticized the IMF during this crisis, including the Nobel Prize-winning economist, Joseph Stiglitz, in his article. 'What I learnt at the world economic crisis.'[12] Today, most of these countries, such as the Asian Tigers – China and India, and other countries in Latin America, can look back at their market liberalization programs with some satisfaction as their economies have grown.

---

12 A more detailed analysis of the Asian Financial Crisis is in the section on the IMF

The beginning of the US hegemony also marked the beginning of the US Dollar as the reserve currency of the world – which meant most international trade was and is still done, in US Dollars. This aspect alone is a huge benefit for the US, which can run high trade deficits without feeling the adverse impacts of these trade deficits. Most of the foreign reserves maintained by central banks around the world are in US Dollars as it is the global currency which helps finance the trade deficit in the US. Most countries, including India and China, maintain large foreign reserves of US Dollars, which are needed to buy petrol and other goods and services in the international market. The US Dollar is also the currency most commodities are priced and traded in. The recent financial meltdown and subsequent large government borrowings in the US, are beginning to undermine the role of the US Dollar as the world's reserve currency.

Nevertheless the US Dollar continues to be the most used currency in the world, with more than 65% of international trade being conducted in it – maintaining its status as the world's reserve currency. There have been calls for an alternative global currency; one which is based on a basket of currencies or on IMF initiated SDRs (Special Drawing Rights). Though there is no clear alternative to the US Dollar as a reserve currency today, countries around the world can and must work towards a global currency that does not give unfair advantage to any one country.

The first three decades after the Second World War were also the years of the Cold War, a time of Balance of Power between the US and the Soviet Union. With the fall of the Soviet Union in 1991, and the dismantling of the Communist regime, the US became the sole super power in the world. The US continues to dominate most aspects of geo-politics in the world with the world's largest economy of more than 14 Trillion Dollars and a military that outspends the militaries of all the major countries in the world combined. The total estimated defense related expenditure for 2009 in the US is said to be close to 1 Trillion USD. The US is a dominant trading country accounting for almost 26-30% of world GDP and trade, though the recent financial crisis has dented it credibility.

The last decade has seen the rise of middle powers such as China, Brazil and India, and a decline in relative US hegemony over many aspects of world politics and business. The quagmire America finds itself in with relation to Afghanistan and Iraq, highlights the limitations of US military power. The dominance of the US military in conventional warfare, which depends on battleships, tanks and advanced aircraft, may be insufficient to tackle the new menace of terrorism. This threat requires a new build-up of capabilities such as urban warfare, covert operations and local intelligence. Middle Powers such as Israel hold the edge in this strategic ability. All these changes in the last decade open up the possibility of a new world order and an opportunity to create a new Balance of Power.

Developments in the last two decades are slowly culminating into major threats to the American dominance of the world. The European Union which is a monetary union of countries in Europe, now has a combined economy of more than 16 Trillion USD, making it the largest economy in the world. The EU market is viewed as a single market in the WTO and the Euro is the second most widely used currency in the world, representing more than 20% of world trade. Mainland EU countries also co-ordinate foreign policy and can pose a legitimate threat to American dominance in world Institutions, even though they mostly adopt similar stances today. China's economy has been growing at more than 9-10% for the past two decades and it now has the second largest economy (for a country), in the world, at more than 4 Trillion USD. China also holds vast amounts of foreign reserves including close to a Trillion dollars of US Government bonds, and is building up its military and space capabilities. The recent financial crisis and subsequent economic downturn in the US has highlighted the imbalance of trade between the US and China. China has raised concerns over the growing fiscal deficit in the US and has questioned the role of the US Dollar as the global reserve currency.

Other growing economies such as Russia, Brazil and India, have seen their influence grow in recent years as they have come out of the global financial crisis much quicker than the US and the EU. India's economy is projected to be the fastest growing economy for the next three decades. Growing ties between the US and India including the civil nuclear pact signed between the two countries, highlights the growing importance of India to the US and on the world stage.

Organizations such as the WTO, can at times provide a counterweight to American policies such as when WTO ruled against the US in a dispute brought on by the EU and other members against US import tariffs on steel, that President Bush imposed through an invocation of section 201 in March of 2002.

Nevertheless, no one country is large enough economically and militarily to challenge the dominance of the US and as such there is no immediate threat to America as the sole super power. As a number of Middle Powers rise in economic and military capabilities, the relative advantage of the US is going to diminish. Even if the economies of China, India, Brazil and others, grow at more than 8% for the next 30 years and the US grows only at 2-3%, they will still be only comparable in size to the US economy, not substantially bigger. Similarly, as the military capabilities around the world improve and catch up with the capabilities of the US military, no one country will be able to dominate the US militarily in the foreseeable future. Therefore, we can safely assume that there is no possibility of a hegemonic war in the next few decades. The only possible strategic choice facing the growing powers and the US, is one based on a Balance of Power in the world.

A Balance of Power in the world between powerful nations can be sustained only through strong world institutions and a just basis of international law, where no one country enjoys special privileges or advantages. There is a strong need to restructure the current set of International institutions such as the UN, IMF, WB etc, which were set up during the hegemonic years of the US, a new world reserve currency, more teeth for International Law and the International Court of Criminal Justice, and trade conventions that benefit all. This transition is not going to be easy but an orderly shift from an era of hegemonic stability to a balance of power is the crucial need of the hour. America realizes the changing shifts of power and is building stronger relations with the growing economies of the world. The civil nuclear pact with India is a sign that the US has acknowledged India as a credible rising power. Its willingness to circumvent NPT and other treaties and laws in providing India with special privileges, is a sign of increased co-operation and the need for a closer relationship with India. Many economists in the US believe that the Chinese Yuan is undervalued by more than 30%, giving exports from China an unfair advantage in global trade. The restraint America has shown in not openly demanding the Yuan be valued up is a sign of both the weakening of US hegemony and the growing importance of diplomatic maneuvering in the balance of power.

India can and should play a key role in this restructuring of the world. As a growing Middle Power with a large population, a fast growing economy and a number of Indian intellectuals in key positions in international institutions, India has the responsibility and ability to shape world institutions and influence the world. India has unique experiences in managing a complex democracy and in restructuring and growing its economy – these are valuable lessons to other growing economies and countries in Asia and Africa. The world view that to date (the last two centuries), has been dominated by Western thought, needs to be tempered by Eastern knowledge and wisdom. There is a need for an Indian Consensus that provides a counter-balance to the Washington Consensus of economic policies and direction at the IMF and the WB. There is the need for India to provide direction at the WTO and to help other developing economies navigate their way through the complex world of global trade. There is a need for India to play the role of a local hegemon in South East Asia and help neighboring countries like Pakistan, Nepal and Bangladesh grow their economies and lift their people out of poverty. There is a need for India to play a role in global issues confronting humanity such as global warming and pollution. There is a need for India and China to play constructive roles in Africa to help lift the continent out of centuries of hardship and exploitation.

In short. a restructuring of the world political and economic systems is imminent. It is imperative for India to play an important role in this restructuring. In order to understand what role India can and should play, we need to clearly outline India's vital, strategic and tactical goals. We must also understand the current state of the world institutions and how they can be shaped for the future.

What are India's Vital, Strategic & Tactical Goals?

India's vital goals include its security and sovereignty, secure borders, the wellbeing of its citizens, domestic tranquillity, and immunity from intimidation – both internal and external. Its strategic goals include gaining access to resources essential to national power; managing and wielding State Power to protect its vital goals and enhance the role India plays on the international stage. Tactical goals include forming alliances; working to ensure WTO negotiations are fair to India and other developing countries; building military capabilities; showcasing cultural identity; and improving the HDI (Human Development Index) of her citizens.

In a speech at the Carnegie Endowment for International Peace, in Washington DC in 2005, the then Indian Minister of Defense, Pranab Mukherjee, outlined four strategic priorities for India based on what he called the Four Deficits: a historical deficit; a security deficit; an economic deficit; and global decision-making deficit[13].

The historical deficit was a reference to the lack of strong ties with countries in the region and especially ties

---

13 www.carnegieendowment.org/files/Mukherjee_Transcript_06-27-051.pdf

with countries with whom India has had strong trade and cultural ties in the past. This deficit needs to be remedied for India to re-establish its regional hegemony. India needs to re-establish strong ties with countries west of India to Central Asia and beyond. India needs to be able to influence events and policies in countries such as Pakistan, Afghanistan, Bangladesh, Myanmar and Sri Lanka. It must also help the economy of the entire region to grow, by opening access to its large market. Regional associations such as SAARC, ASEAN etc, need to be more influential and capable of creating a stable and growing region. India also has vital interests in the Gulf which is an important source of energy as well as home to over 3.5 million Indians, who work and live there. India has traditionally had strong relationships with Iraq and Iran, which are currently facing their own external and internal crises. It is important for India to re-establish and maintain strong ties to countries in the Gulf.

The security deficit has two major components — one being the threat India faces on its external borders, and the other is its internal Maoist and other insurgencies which destabilize peace and security. India faces threats on its borders from two fronts – Pakistan and China. The skirmishes on the borders typically involve low-intensity weaponry but can escalate into bigger conflicts employing artillery and other heavy weaponry such as used in Kargil. Both China and Pakistan have nuclear weapons and the internal turmoil in Pakistan is a major cause for concern with fears of low-grade and other nuclear weapons falling into the hands of terrorists, which could be used against densely populated Indian cities. State sponsored terrorism from Pakistan is also a major threat to India's internal peace. A number of terrorist attacks in India, including attacks on its parliament, prominent hotels and other locations, are serious breaches which must be tackled and stopped with a combination of hard and soft power. China has upgraded its military and navy in recent decades. It now has vastly superior military strength and capabilities. Unresolved borders with China in the north-east of India, pose serious security threats to India. Though India has nuclear capabilities, a lot of planning and re-thinking on modern military strategy has to be undertaken by the Indian Army.

Future wars will look very different from those of the past. Over-reliance on traditional equipment such as tanks and large armies, may be counterproductive. India needs precision strike capabilities, coupled with a strong intelligence network and both personnel and hardware to tackle low-intensity conflicts. A special focus on urban warfare is needed to counter terrorist activities. The second major security deficit is India's lack of a coherent strategy to deal with its internal Naxalite and Maoist threats. Vast areas of the country are under-developed and provide fertile breeding grounds for these movements which threaten domestic security and peace. A combination of social, economic and police/military strategies are required to overcome this problem.

On the 6th April 2010, Maoist rebels ambushed a contingent of the Federal Central Reserve Police Force (CRPF), who were conducting a domination exercise in Dantewada, in the central Indian state of Chattisgarh, and killed 76 policemen – the deadliest attack by the Maoists on Indian security forces. This attack not only demonstrated the capabilities of the Maoists but also exposed the serious lack of training, discipline and weapons of the CRPF *jawans* (soldiers) in the fight against the Maoists. On the social aspects of the problem, this insurgency has been argued to be a response to the commercial exploitation of the forest regions which are home to tribal populations – resulting in widespread loss of livelihood and exploitation. These regions also are very under-developed with low levels of literacy. In 2009, Prime Minister Manmohan Singh declared that the Maoists pose the largest internal threat to India's security. The Indian government has responded with Operation Greenhunt – a counter offensive with more than 50,000 paramilitary troops. But any strategy must include social and economic development of the region. India needs to be able to overcome these internal and external security threats to further its vital and strategic goals and be taken seriously on the international stage.

With reference to the economic deficit, Pranab Mukherjee outlined three major aspects: energy, technology and agriculture. India is a heavily energy deficient country. More than 70% of its crude oil requirements are met through imports. Of all the variables that can hinder India's economic growth, energy dependence is probably the most serious of the deficiencies as economic growth and energy consumption are highly correlated. India needs long-term alternatives to oil to meet its energy requirements. One of the most attractive options is nuclear energy.

The signing of the Indo-US Civilian Nuclear Agreement in 2009, is a step in this direction. The 45 nation Nuclear Suppliers Group (NSG), granted a waiver to India, allowing it to access civilian nuclear technology and fuel from other countries, making India the only known country with nuclear weapons which is not a party to the Non-Proliferation Treaty (NPT), but is still allowed to carry out nuclear commerce with the rest of the world. India also needs to develop other non-renewable sources of energy such as solar and wind. The recent National Solar Mission is a positive step in this direction.

In the area of conventional energy sources, India is competing against China and other growing economies in acquiring petroleum-related assets in Africa, Russia and other parts of the world. While IT (Information Technology)-related companies in India have made a mark on the global economy, India still lags behind the developed world in a number of advanced technologies, and is dependent on foreign sources of technology and knowledge. This is a deficit that must be remedied for India to break out of the dependency or satellite mode of development and become a leader in the world economy.

With regard to agricultural deficit (this sector remains India's main source of livelihood), the sector suffers from low productivity and a lack of access to the global market. Subsistence farming is an impediment to efficiency and could be a long-term threat to India's food security. More research is required in developing technologies suitable to India's climate, soil and food requirements, as well as access to markets in developed countries which will provide the necessary impetus to the sector.

India has to show leadership at the WTO talks to help gain access to these markets – which will not only benefit farmers in India but also a majority of the developing and underdeveloped countries that depend heavily on their agricultural sectors. There is no question that India must continue on the path of liberalization and work on growing its economy at a rate greater than 8-9%, to pull millions of Indians out of poverty and subsistence living standards.

Economic growth is essential to improving living conditions and in securing vital goals for the wellbeing of its citizens and to build State Power.

The final strategic priority and a current deficit, is global decision-making or India's place (or lack of), in the major decision-making bodies of the world. India has a small and limited role in a majority of these bodies. We will explore this topic in more detail in the next few chapters. While the first three deficits are important topics and can each occupy the contents of an entire book, my focus here is on India's global decision-making deficit.

As we have discussed, the world is undergoing enormous changes in its geo-political-economic structures and the relationships between nations. We are on the cusp of a new world order. A new system of world institutions, built on a global balance of power and the fair, equitable and just basis of international law, will evolve in the coming decades. India can and should play an important role in this restructuring of world institutions and secure an important place in the world. The next few chapters are dedicated to understanding the current state of world institutions such as the UN, IMF, WB, WTO and the impact they have on nations of the world, as well as the direction of their future evolution and what India's role should be in these institutions.

THE UNITED NATIONS
& INDIA'S PLACE IN THE WORLD

2

The idea of global peace or 'one world family', is deeply felt and built into the conscience of Indians. The *Vedas* defined the concept of *Vasudhaiva Kutumbakam* or the entire world as one family, many millennia ago.

*Ayam **bandhurayam neti** gananā laghuchetasām*
Udāracharitānām tu vasudhaiva kutumbakam
One is my brother and the other is not – is the thinking of a narrow-minded person. For those who are broad-minded, liberals, or noble people, the entire world is a one big family. *~ Maha Upanishad Ch 6:72*

The world view espoused by ancient India was based on *Loka Samasta Sukhina Bhavantu*, which can be translated as 'Let the entire world be happy'. A number of Hindu concepts such as *dharma* and *ahimsa*, were developed as a basis of human conduct for the ideals of human unity and a world free from conflict and misery to exist. India's foreign policy immediately after independence can be viewed as a modern day interpretation and application of this ancient philosophy. Jawaharlal Nehru, the first Prime Minister of Independent India, espoused principles such as the Panchsheel or the five principles of peaceful coexistence, in a series of agreements with the People's Republic of China. The five principles which are: Mutual respect for each other's territorial integrity and sovereignty; Mutual non-aggression against anyone; Mutual non-interference in each other's internal affairs; Equality and mutual benefit; and Peaceful co-existence, were also the basis of the Non-Aligned Movement started by India under Nehru's leadership.

In the West, by contrast, peace was a state of affairs during which conflict was minimized or eliminated by a great power or hegemon which was supremely dominant and weaker states dared not attack or provoke a war. A good example from first and second century AD, is the early Roman Empire established by Caesar Augustus, which brought in long periods of relative peace and few conflicts, also called *Pax Romana* or *Pax Augusta*. Augustus created a junta of the greatest military leaders and by creating a coalition of the strongest magnates, eliminated the prospect of civil war in the empire. Great Britain, during the 19th and 20th centuries (1815-1914), controlled most of the key naval trade routes and enjoyed unchallenged sea power and was able to establish a period of relative peace in Europe, also sometimes referred to as *Pax Britannica*. Britain established an empire that circled the globe and she was the dominant power until the First World War in 1914. Others including King Henry IV of France, who created alliances with a view to establishing peace based on the same idea of a dominant country and by virtue of its superior power.

The modern day Western view and strategies for world peace can be traced back to Immanuel Kant's 1795 essay titled, 'Perpetual Peace: A philosophical Sketch'[14]. Kant described his proposed peace program as containing two steps – the Preliminary Articles, which include:

1. No secret treaty of peace shall be held valid in which there is tacitly reserved matter for a future war
2. No independent states, large or small, shall come under the dominion of another state by inheritance, exchange, purchase or donation
3. Standing armies shall in time be totally abolished
4. National debts shall not be contracted with a view to the external friction of states
5. No state shall by force interfere with the constitution or government of another state
6. No state shall, during war, permit such acts of hostility which would make mutual confidence in the subsequent peace impossible.

And the Definitive Articles, which form the foundation on which peace can be built and which include:

1. The civil constitution of every state should be republican or have a representative government
2. The law of nations shall be founded on a federation of free states
3. The law of world citizenship shall be limited to conditions of universal hospitality

The strategy is based on three ideas: democratic or representative governments are more pacific than other forms of government; commerce makes war unprofitable, or as Joseph Schumpeter argued, capitalism makes modern states inherently peaceful; and that a confederation or

---

14 http://www.mtholyoke.edu/acad/intrel/kant/kant1.htm

league of nations could produce perpetual peace. He argued that a league of nations or an international community of free and democratic states bound by trade and commerce, with common interests, could promote and preserve a peaceful society worldwide. The first such international organization was the League of Nations.

THE LEAGUE OF NATIONS

By the beginning of the 20th century, Britain was no longer a dominant hegemon and two power blocs emerged through alliances between different powers in Europe. Tensions over territory in the Balkans and alliances between various powers in Europe, drew the entire continent into the First World War in 1914. This was the first major war in Europe between industrialized countries which had massively built up their war capabilities through mass production, and it resulted in unprecedented casualties and destruction of life and property. By the time the war ended in 1918, it had a profound impact and anti-war sentiments rose across the world. The creation of an international organization whose aim was to prevent war through disarmament, open diplomacy and international co-operation, was seen as the best possible way to prevent future conflict. The then US President, Woodrow Wilson, promoted the idea of the League of Nations as a means of avoiding future world conflicts and the creation of the League of Nations was a centerpiece of Wilson's Fourteen Points for Peace.

The Paris Peace Conference which took place between the Allied victors in 1919, following the end of World War 1, set the peace terms for Germany and its allies. It was also at this conference that the League of Nations was created. Forty-four States signed the Covenant of the League of Nations in 1919 and despite the efforts of Wilson to establish and promote the League (for which he was awarded the Nobel Peace Prize), the US did not join the League due to opposition in the US Senate from the Republicans[15]. The League's primary goals, as stated in its Covenant, include preventing war through collective security, disarmament and the settling of international disputes through negotiation and arbitration.

The League of Nations was established with three main constitutional organs: The Assembly; the Council; and the Permanent Secretariat. The relations between the Assembly and the Council were not explicitly defined but unanimity of decision between the Assembly and the Council was required before a resolution could be adopted.

The Assembly consisted of representatives from all members of the League and each nation had one vote. The special functions of the Assembly included admission of new members, the periodical election of non-permanent members to the Council and control of the budget.

The League Council acted as a type of executive body directing the Assembly's business and began with four permanent members (Great Britain, France, Italy and Japan). The composition of the Council changed a number of times and finally had 11 non-permanent members. Germany became the fifth permanent member of the Council in 1926, but soon left the League, along with Japan.

---

15 Historians have attributed two reasons for this, one being that Wilson kept the draft of the proposed league secret until the peace conference and never consulted with Republicans on the draft and the second that Wilson made the League the major issue of the Democratic congressional campaign in 1918 which aroused violent opposition from Republican opponents and Senator Lodge a former Republican supporter of the League led the opposition to it. Republicans won control of both the house and senate in the elections and the treaty was rejected twice in the senate.

The Permanent Secretariat, established at the seat of the League in Geneva, comprised of a body of experts under the direction of the General Secretary.

The League also oversaw the Court of International Justice and several other agencies and commissions, such as the Health Organization, the ILO and the commission for Refugees, created to deal with pressing international problems. Several of these institutions were transferred to the UN after the Second World War.

The outbreak of the Second World War exposed the ineffectiveness of the League of Nations in its primary purpose of avoiding global conflicts. One of the key reasons for this ineffectiveness can be attributed to the lack of a single dominant power or coalition which could make the League effective. Some have argued that the presence of the US in the League, which along with the UK and France, could have built a powerful coalition, but the absence of the US led to the eventual collapse of the League. There were other issues including the requirements of a unanimous vote of its member Council and the Assembly, which led to the League being ineffective. The League's supposed neutrality also slowed the decision-making process and nationalist fears among nations caused many of them not to join the League or to leave it quickly. Japan, which began as a permanent member of the Council, withdrew in 1933, after the League voiced opposition to its invasion of the Chinese territory of Manchuria. Italy, which also began as a permanent member, withdrew in 1937, and though the League admitted Germany as a member in 1926, Adolf Hitler pulled Germany out when he came to power in 1933.

This lack of representation also hurt the League's

ability to preserve peace. Ultimately the League failed in its primary purpose of preventing another World War and the onset of the Second World War led to the demise of the League of Nations. At the 1943 Tehran Conference, the Allied Powers agreed to create a new body to replace the League – the United Nations. Many League bodies such as the ILO, became affiliated with the UN. The final meeting of the League of Nations was held on 12 April 1946, in Geneva. The motion that dissolved the League passed unanimously.

India was still a part of the British Empire during the time of the League of Nations and was one of the original signatories for its role and contribution to the Allies in the war. In the Assembly of the League in 1928, the leader of the Indian delegation, the Nawab of Palanpur, brought up and emphasized the topic of racial equality. He argued that the League itself was based on the concept of universal equality and that the idea of 'equal obligations and equal rights' should be entitled to all races. Japan was a strong advocate of the racial equality principle as well and made it the subject of one its proposals at the peace conference. The League also sent technical missions and experts to advise the government on various topics including a Malaria Commission to tackle the disease. India's role at the League can be summed up as being of little significance except for the participation of Indian intellectuals at the various technical organizations and India's ambition to become a non-permanent member on the Council.

THE UNITED NATIONS

The outbreak of the Second World War heralded the demise of the League of Nations. As the war raged in Europe between Britain, France and the Allies and the Axis nations of Germany, Italy and Japan, the British Prime

Minister, Winston Churchill, and the US President, Franklin D. Roosevelt, meet aboard warships and issued a joint declaration in August of 1941. This declaration, also known as the Atlantic Charter[16], set out the goals and aims of the Allied powers concerning the war and the post-war world and the conditions based on which the US would provide material support to Britain against Nazi aggression. (The US had not joined the war yet and was reluctant to take part.)

The Atlantic Charter had eight main points:

1. No territorial gains were to be sought by the US or the UK.
2. Territorial adjustments must be in accord with the wishes of the peoples concerned.
3. All peoples had a right to self-determination.
4. Trade barriers were to be lowered with emphasis that both victor and vanquished would be given market access on equal terms.
5. There was to be global economic cooperation and advancement of social welfare.
6. Freedom from want and fear.
7. Freedom of the seas.
8. Disarmament of aggressor nations and common disarmament.

Many historians have argued that the punitive damages sought by the victorious allied powers in World War I caused so much suffering and antipathy in Germany, that it led to the rise of Hitler and a strong nationalist fervor that led to the Second World War. The Atlantic Charter spelt out in no uncertain terms that the mistakes made by the victors of

---

16   http://www.archives.gov/education/lessons/fdr-churchill/images/atlantic-charter.gif

World War I would not be repeated after the Second World War. Also, the acknowledgement that all peoples had the right to self determination, gave hope to independence leaders in British colonies, including India, that their demands for national autonomy would be granted when the war ended.

Churchill dismissed such ideas quickly and in a speech in September 1941, he rejected its applicability to nations in the British Colonial Empire, such as India. President Roosevelt chose to support the British position, which generated strong anti-American feelings in India and led many to complain of double standards. Gandhi, in a letter to president Roosevelt in 1942, wrote, "I venture to think that the Allied declaration that the allies are fighting to make the world safe for the freedom of the individual and for democracy sounds hollow so long as India and for that matter Africa are exploited by Great Britain."[17] The acceptance of the principle of self-determination nevertheless accelerated decolonization movements in Asia and Africa and soon many countries gained their independence, including India in 1947 – two years after the end of the Second World War.

The Atlantic Charter formed the basis of the United Nations and also marked the transition of power from Britain to the United States. Soon after the Atlantic Charter was signed, the Japanese attacked Pearl Harbor in December 1941. That drew the US into the Second World War. US President, Franklin D. Roosevelt, first coined the term 'United Nations', to describe the Allied countries. It was first officially used on 1 January 1942, when 26 governments signed the

---

17 Kanishkan Sathasivam, *Uneasy neighbors: India, Pakistan, and US foreign policy*, p. 59 (Google books)

Atlantic Charter, pledging to continue the war effort. The United Nations thus began its journey as a wartime alliance of the Allies fighting the Second World War.

A series of conferences, beginning with the Washington Conversations on International Peace and Security Organization also known as the Dumbarton Oaks Conference in August 1944, where the make-up of the UN including which States would be invited to become members; the formation of the UN Security Council; and the right of veto to be given to permanent members of the Security Council; were discussed, was followed by the Yalta Conference in February 1945, and culminated in the United Nations Conference on International Organization (UNCIO), or the San Francisco Conference, in April 1945. At the UNCIO, there were delegates from more than 50 Allied nations and the conference resulted in the creation of the United Nations Charter.

After the war ended with the Americans using atomic weapons against the Japanese, the US emerged as one of the most dominant powers in the world and helped establish the international system including the UN and its various organizations, which remain more or less unchanged to this day. Harry Truman, who was the Vice President of the US, succeeded to the presidency in 1945, when President Roosevelt died less than three months after beginning his fourth term. Both President Roosevelt and Truman made sure that the mistakes made by President Wilson were not repeated and they included both the Democrats and the Republicans in the discussions leading up to the creation of the UN Charter. The US was the first country to ratify the new UN Charter. Both were very supportive of the UN which led to optimism for the new organization, as one of the reasons for the failure of the League of Nations was attributed to the lack of US participation.

The UN Charter shared a number of similarities with the covenants of the League and included:

1. The major purpose was to maintain peace and security and to take collective measures to implement that aim.
2. Its basic organization consisted of a general assembly open to all members, a security council made up of the major powers and the permanent secretariat.
3. The UN inherited a number of the social and economic organizations that coordinated activities worldwide such as the WHO and the ILO.

The major differences, which have helped sustain the UN since its foundation include:

1. Universal membership.
2. Voting in the Security Council and other UN bodies not by unanimity but by majority.
3. More flexibility in dealing with international issues
4. A lot more emphasis on social and economic affairs.
5. Most importantly, the support and the backing of the USA.

Today, the UN has 192 member States (every sovereign state in the world except for the City State of the Vatican, which is a permanent observer), and is constituted of five active bodies: The General Assembly, The Security

Council, The Secretariat, The Economic and Social Council and the International Court of Justice[18]. The UN Trusteeship Council which was the sixth body at the time of founding, is no longer active. The Economic and Social Council oversees a number of prominent agencies such as the World Health Organization (WHO), the World Food Program (WFP), the International Labor Organization (ILO), the UN Educational Scientific and Culture Organization (UNESCO), the UN Development Program (UNDP) and the UN Conference on Trade and Development (UNCTAD).

The General Assembly is made up of all the members of the UN and is the main deliberative and policy-making forum. All members have the opportunity to address the assembly and the work of the UN year round derives largely from mandates given by the General Assembly. It also plays a significant role in the process of standards-setting and the process of creating international law. The major provisions in the UN Charter for the General Assembly[19] are:

1. Article 10 – the General Assembly may make recommendations on any matters within the scope of the charter.
2. Article 12 – It may discuss and make recommendations on questions relating to peace and security provided the dispute is not being considered by the Security Council unless the Security Council so requests.
3. Article 11 – Gives the General Assemble the responsibility of making recommendations on the regulation of armaments.
4. Article 13 – Indicates that it should make

18 http://www.un.org/aboutun/chart_en.pdf
19 http://www.un.org/en/documents/charter/index.shtml

recommendations on promoting international cooperation in economic, social and related fields.
5. Article 15 – It should receive and review annual reports from the Security Council and other organs of the UN.
6. Article 17 gives the Assembly the authority to approve the budget and apportion expenses.
7. Discussions on important matters including the budget need a 2/3 majority while other only need a simple majority.

The Security Council has the primary responsibility of maintaining international peace and security. The Security Council is the only organ of the UN that can make binding decisions that member governments have to carry out under the terms of the Charter Article 25. This makes the UN Security Council the most powerful body in the UN Organization and in international politics. There are five permanent members of the Security Council, including the US, UK, France, China and Russia. These permanent members also enjoy veto power or the power to unilaterally block, any Security Council resolution. The Council also has 10 non-permanent members voted in by the General Assembly on a regional basis and who hold two-year terms. Whereas the General Assembly meets only for a couple of months every year from September, the Security Council is designed to function continuously throughout the year. The major provisions in the UN Charter for the Security Council[20] are:

1. Articles 30-42 provide for deciding on measures including economic and military pressure to maintain and restore international peace and

---

20 http://www.un.org/en/documents/charter/chapter5.shtml

security. Members of the UN agree to make available armed forces and facilities for this purpose but are subject to ratification by the states involved. (The US Congress has the constitutional right to approve or oppose the President's use of force.)

2. Article 47 provides for a military staff committee under the Security Council for strategic direction of any armed forces placed at the disposal of the UNSC.
3. Article 51 states that nothing in the charter shall impair a member's right of individual or collective self defense if an attack occurs against a member of the UN but this shall not affect the authority of the UNSC.

The UN Secretariat is headed by the Secretary-General, the most visible face of the UN Organization and has a staff of civil servants worldwide. It provides research information, studies and facilities, needed by UN bodies, and carries out tasks as directed by them. Its services include surveying economic and social trends and preparing studies on human rights, among others. It is also responsible for administering peacekeeping operations and in mediating international disputes

The Economic and Social Council is the principal organ to co-ordinate the economic and social work of the UN and oversees the work of numerous specialized agencies and institutions around the world for promoting international co-operation for economic and social problems. Eighty percentage of the UN system's budget is overseen by the ESSOC, and the various organizations and institutions under it perform important social and economic work throughout the world. The main goals of ESSOC[21] are:

---

21 http://www.un.org/en/ecosoc/about/index.shtml

1. Promoting higher standards of living, full employment and economic and social progress
2. Identifying solutions to international economic, social and health problems.
3. Facilitating international cultural and educational cooperation.
4. Encouraging universal respect for human rights and fundamental freedoms.

The International Court of Justice, located in The Hague, Netherlands, is the principal judicial organ of the UN. It settles legal disputes between States and advises the UN on international matters. The International Court hears cases related to war crimes, ethnic cleansing and disputes between nations.

An important aspect of running the operations of the UN is funding the costs of the various organizations and their activities. While the General Assembly is authorized to approve the budget and apportion expenses, the source of funding comes from the member nations both from assessed and voluntary contributions. Assessed contributions finance the regular budgets of the UN, the specialized agencies and the IAEA, and the assessed contribution is one of the legal obligations accepted by a country when it joins the UN. Most UN peacekeeping operations are also funded through special assessed accounts. The assessments for each member are broadly based on their capacity to pay as measured by their Gross National Income (GNI), with adjustments for external debt and per capita income. Voluntary contributions finance special programs and offices created by the UN, such as the WHO, and no country is legally obliged to contribute to these programs. Voluntary contributions currently make up for than 50% of the entire UN systems budget[22].

---

22 http://www.unjiu.org/data/reports/2007/en2007_01.pdf

The UN General Assembly has also established 'ceiling' rates, setting the maximum amount any member can be assessed, which is currently at 22%, and the minimum amount assessed is at 0.001% of the UN budget[23]. The US is the only country that is assessed at the maximum rate of 22%, and contributes a substantial 22% of UN's general budget. The top five countries that contribute to the UN Budget are the US, Japan, Germany, UK and France, who together make up more than 60% of the total budget. India contributes less than .5% of the UN's budget (assessed at 0.45% of the budget), and net contributions in 2009 were a mere 10.9 Million USD. In contrast, Mexico, which has a GDP equivalent in size to that of India, contributes 2.257% of the UN's budget and had a net contribution in 2009, of close to 55 Million USD, or almost five times India's contribution. Even the small Island nation of Singapore, contributes almost 0.35% of the UN budget, with net contributions of over 8 million USD. The current operating budget of the UN (excluding the peacekeeping budget and budget for all other UN programs such as the WHO, UNDP etc), is estimated at $4.19 Billion for a 2-year period or a little over 2 Billion USD per year[24]. The peacekeeping budget is over $5 Billion, with some 70,000 troops deployed in 17 missions around the world.

Funding for special UN programs such as the WHO, is voluntary, and many of these agencies suffer from severe shortages during economic recessions – such as the World Food Program (WFP) being forced to cut services in 2009-2010, due to insufficient funding. There is a serious crisis in Niger, Chad, Guinea and other countries in West Africa,

23 http://globalpolicy.org/images/pdfs/Member_States_Assessment_for_Regular_Budget_for_2010.pdf
24 Source: un.org and http://www.un.org/ga/search/view_doc.asp?symbol=ST/ADM/SER.B/755

where acute malnutrition in children under the age of five has reached an alarming 17% of the population, but the UN response has been poor as the UN Office for the Co-ordination of Humanitarian Affairs (OCHA), has been severely under-funded by almost two-thirds of its budget of $500 Million. Most UN agencies are suffering from budget shortfalls, including UNICEF, which is struggling to find funding to vaccinate children against measles and other diseases leading to child mortality, in Africa. This has led to a major measles outbreak, a preventable disease, in eastern and southern Africa, affecting more than 47,000 children in 14 countries.[25] Low levels of funding for the World Food Program is threatening vital child feeding programs in Yemen and other countries facing a severe hunger crises.

In December 2009, the WFP had to cut the amount of food aid it could provide to the poorest areas in Nepal and restored it only after the Department for International Development (DFID) of the UK, donated $8 million and the UN Central Emergency Response Fund released $6 million for operations in Nepal[26]. It is important to note that India contributes a very small percentage of WFP's budget, at a little over 1 million USD, while Brazil (a country in the same league), contributes more than 14 times more. Even Bangladesh contributed twice what India did, at $2.29 million.[27] If India wants to be taken seriously on the international stage, it must do more and play a bigger and more active leadership role in these institutions to help solve humanitarian and other crises around the world, especially

25 http://157.150.195.10/apps/news/story.asp?NewsID=35073&Cr=measles&Cr1=

26 http://www.nepalnews.com/main/index.php/news-archive/19-general/3807-wfp-receives-donations-to-support-12m-people-in-nepal.html

27 http://documents.wfp.org/stellent/groups/public/documents/research/wfp216777.pdf

those in India's backyard – in countries like Nepal and Myanmar, that need help. Before India can be a world leader, it must demonstrate its leadership abilities and willingness to take charge in its region (South East Asia) and must be able to act responsibly as a regional power/hegemon.

THE IMPACT OF THE UN ON THE WORLD – SUCCESSES & FAILURES OF COLLECTIVE SECURITY

The UN has played an important role in the decolonization of the world. When it was formed in 1945, over one-third of the world's population lived in colonies of Western powers. That figure has now gone down to almost zero. The right of self-determination that was first written into the Atlantic Charter and later incorporated into the UN Charter, Chapter XI: Articles 73 & 74), gave a strong impetus to the decolonization movement. The General Assembly adopted Resolution 1514[28], also known as the Declaration on the Granting of Independence to Colonial Countries and Peoples, in 1960. This declaration stated that all people have a right to self-determination and proclaimed that colonialism should be brought to a speedy and unconditional end. The UN General Assembly also created the Special Committee on Decolonization in 1961, for the purpose of monitoring implementation of the Declaration on the Granting of Independence to Colonial Countries and Peoples, and to make recommendations on its application. The UN Charter binds colonizing powers to recognize the interests of their colonies; to agree to promote social, economic, political and educational progress; and to assist in developing appropriate forms of self-government. Since the creation of the UN, more than 80 former colonies have gained independence.[29] In 1990, the General Assembly

---

28 http://www.undemocracy.com/A-RES-1514(XV).pdf
29 http://www.un.org/Depts/dpi/decolonization/history.htm

proclaimed 1990-2000 as the International Decade for the Eradication of Colonialism.

The Korean War: the UN was at the centre of action during the Korean War in 1950. Korea was annexed by Japan in 1910. Subsequent to Japan's defeat in the Second World War and in line with the principles of the Atlantic Charter, the US and the Soviet Union agreed that Korea should be given its independence after the war. After the War ended, a conference was convened in Moscow, in 1945, to discuss the future of Korea and a 5-year-four-power-trusteeship was proposed. But due to the politics of the Cold War, hopes of a unified and independent Korea soon evaporated, resulting in the establishment of a Communist North and a Democratic South Korea. Korea was divided into North and South Korea at the 38th parallel. In November 1947, US President, Harry Truman, tabled the Korean issue at the UN General Assembly, which created a nine-member commission to establish an all Korean government.

The Soviet bloc boycotted these meetings and refused permission for the Commission to enter North Korea. The Commission arranged for elections in the South and the UN General Assembly recognized South Korea as the only lawful government in Korea. The UN General Assembly then established another Commission to bring about unification, which stayed in South Korea to observe developments. This Commission, on 25 June 1950, informed the UN General Secretary that North Korean forces had attacked the Republic of South Korea all along the 38th parallel. On the same day, the UN Security Council, at the request of the US and by a unanimous vote, called for immediate cessation of hostilities and the withdrawal of North Korean forces.

Two days later, the UNSC adopted a US resolution calling on all members to furnish all necessary assistance to repel the armed attack and announced that it had ordered land and sea forces to support South Korea. The UNSC also passed a resolution requesting the US to command UN forces, and authorizing them to operate under the UN flag. Combat units for the unified command were provided by a number of countries and a truly international force was created to combat the troops from North Korea.

China did not participate in the Korean attack initially but as the UN troops crossed the 38th parallel into North Korea, Chinese troops entered the war (as independents, so as to not provoke an all out war with the US), which ended when the Armistice agreement was signed in 1953. There has been no permanent settlement of this conflict and the US maintains a sizeable number of troops along the border. The US also continued to report periodically to the Security Council on the implementation of the Armistice agreement. Most observers regard the UN action to defend South Korea as a high point in supporting collective security under the UN Charter. It is important to keep in mind the actions of the US, the dominant power of the capitalist world, in the success of this UN mission. It reflects the fact that the UN needs the support of major powers that are capable and willing to act in order to carry out its mission.

The Vietnam War: in contrast to the Korean War, the war in Vietnam exposed the limitations of the collective security arrangement supported by the UN and the Security Council. After World War II, a Communist insurgency led by Hi Chi Minh, fought the French, trying to end their colonial rule. In 1954, after being defeated by the Communist forces, France negotiated the Geneva Agreements with North Vietnam.

These provided for the establishment of the Democratic Republic of Vietnam in the North and a government in the South under Emperor Bao Dai, but specified no role for the UN. South Vietnam was then formally recognized by over 90 nations – most countries outside the Communist bloc – while the Communist nations formally recognized North Vietnam and the position that Vietnam should be unified under the Communist government of the North.

In 1964, US President, Lyndon Johnson, requested an urgent meeting of the UNSC, complaining that US vessels were being attacked by North Vietnam in international waters. Any action was blocked by the possibility of a Soviet veto and the conflict between the North and the South, supported by the US, escalated with the US eventually sending more than 500,000 of its own troops. The then Secretary General of the UN,   U Thant, in an annual report to the General Assembly, explained why the UN would not take further steps to end the war. He noted the Geneva agreements of 1954 prescribed no role for the UN, and that neither North nor South Vietnam was a UN member. Neither party involved was willing to discuss or negotiate. Action from the UNSC was absent due to the veto power of the Soviet Union. North Vietnam was determined to unify the country under its control, which it eventually did in 1975, after the US had withdrawn its forces from South Vietnam. The UN was virtually powerless in this war and neither side was willing to yield.

The Middle East: in contrast to the relative success of the Korean War and the failure of the US and South Vietnam in the Vietnam War, the Middle East wars have been long and painful, with no decision. The UN has been in the centre of action since the first war in 1948. A special UN committee and the General Assembly, decided to split Palestine into two states – the Jewish state of Israel and the Arab state of Palestine, in 1948. Arab nations were opposed to this solution and major wars followed. The first in 1956, was started by France, Britain and Israel, with the aim of forcing Egypt to give back the Suez Canal, which it had nationalized. The second war was triggered when Egypt mobilized to threaten Israel, and third was initiated in 1973, when Egypt attacked to regain territory lost in the 1967 war.

In each case the wars were ended with mediation within the UN framework, with the help of UN peacekeeping forces, and with major political and material assistance by the US and other major powers. In 1978 and again in 1983, Israel invaded Lebanon to retaliate against terrorists and to force the PLO (Palestine Liberation Organization of Yasser Arafat) out. The Israelis, under pressure from the US and with the support of UN peacekeeping forces along the border of Syria (UNDOF) and UN patrols in Southern Lebanon (UNIFIL), withdrew their troops from Lebanon. UNDOF (United Nations Disengagement Observer Force), was established in 1974, by UN Security Council resolution 350 (1974)[30], following the agreed disengagement of Israeli and Syrian forces in the Golan Heights. It continues to supervise the implementation of the disengagement agreement. UNIFIL, which was established by the UN Security Council in 1978, by its resolution 425 (1978) and 426 (1978), continues to monitor the border to this day. Following the July/ August 2006 Israeli-Hezbollah War, the Security Council, by resolution 1701 (2006)[31], has significantly enhanced UNIFIL and expanded its original mandate.

---

30 http://www.un.org/en/peacekeeping/missions/undof/
31 http://www.un.org/en/peacekeeping/missions/unifil/mandate.shtml

End of the Cold War & the Role of America in International Peace & Security: the break-up of the Soviet Union in 1991, signalled the end of the Cold War and the emergence of the United States as the sole super power in the world. Since then, the US has led a number of international conflicts, sometimes with UNSC authorization and at other times unilaterally or with a coalition of partners outside the UNSC process. Significant actions include the first Gulf War against Saddam Hussein's attack on Kuwait; the Kosovo War to stop genocide; the war in Afghanistan against the terrorist group Al Qaeda and their Taliban supporters; and the Iraq War, which was controversial with even some allies of the US such as France, opposing it.

The First Gulf War: the Persian Gulf War or Gulf War, was a UN authorized response to Iraq's invasion of Kuwait in August 1990. Within hours of the invasion, Kuwaiti and US delegations requested a meeting of the UNSC, which passed Resolution 660, condemning the invasion and demanding withdrawal of Iraqi troops[32]. The following day, the Arab League passed its own resolution which called for a solution to the conflict from within the League and warned against outside intervention.

A few days later, the UNSC passed Resolution 661[33], and placed economic sanctions on Iraq. UNSC Resolution 665 followed, which authorized a naval blockade to enforce the economic sanctions against Iraq. Soon after his conquest of Kuwait, Hussein began verbally attacking the Saudi Kingdom. US President, H.W. Bush, soon announced that the US would launch a wholly defensive mission to prevent Iraq from invading Saudi Arabia, under the

---

32 http://www.unhcr.org/refworld/docid/3b00f12240.html
33 http://www.unhcr.org/refworld/docid/3b00f16b24.html

codename *Operation Desert Shield*. The wholly defensive doctrine was abandoned when Iraq declared Kuwait to be the 19th province of Iraq and Ali Hassan was appointed its military governor.

The UNSC Resolution 678, passed in November 1990, gave Iraq a withdrawal deadline of 15 January, 1991, and authorized 'all necessary means to uphold and implement Resolution 660', as well as the use of force, if Iraq failed to comply. The US assembled a coalition force to implement Resolution 678, with personnel from 34 countries. The US contributed the maximum number of troops and resources for the effort. A day after the deadline set in Resolution 678, the coalition forces launched a massive air campaign and *Operation Desert Storm* had officially begun. The ground assault began a few weeks later and the coalition forces registered a decisive victory, liberating Kuwait and enforcing collective security in the region. However, they did not move into Baghdad or remove Saddam and this set the stage for the Iraq War a few years later.

The Afghanistan War: on 11 September 2001, Al Qaeda terrorists hijacked four commercial planes. In a suicide mission, the terrorists flew the planes into the World Trade Center buildings in New York and the Pentagon Building in Arlington, Virginia, killing everyone on board the flights. The impact of the collisions and subsequent fires, brought down the twin towers, killing many others. A fourth plane that the hijackers had intended to crash into the US Capitol, crashed into fields near Shanksville, in rural Pennsylvania. In addition to the 19 hijackers, a total of 2995 people died in what many described as the single deadliest attack on US soil in living memory. The US responded by launching the War on Terrorism, with the stated goals of bringing

Osama bin Laden and Al Qaeda to justice. The strategy also included preventing the emergence of other terrorist networks, using any means necessary, including economic and military sanctions against States perceived as harboring terrorists. That day changed everything for US foreign policy and led to the creation of the Bush Doctrine, including the controversial policy of preventive war; a policy of spreading democracy around the world, especially in the Middle East; a strategy for combating terrorism; and a willingness to pursue US military interests unilaterally.

The first response to these attacks was the war in Afghanistan to overthrow the Taliban regime, which provided safe haven to Al Qaeda, and to capture Osama bin Laden and bring him to justice. The US military's *Operation Enduring Freedom* was launched in October 2001, with coalition forces that included troops from the UK, Australia and other NATO Allies of the US. The UN did not authorize the US-led invasion of Afghanistan but the US has argued that UNSC authorization was not required since the invasion was an act of collective self-defense provided for under Article 51 of the UN Charter. The US also had international opinion and sympathy for its operations in Afghanistan.

The Taliban fled Kabul in November 2001, and from the southern city of Kandahar by December 2001. The primary or preliminary stage of the war was over. To fill the political void, the UN hosted the Bonn Conference in 2001, which resulted in the Bonn Agreement, that created the Afghan Interim Authority. To provide security for this Interim Authority, the UN authorized an international force – the International Security Assistance Force (ISAF) – which included soldiers from 42 countries, with US troops making up half its force. Later in 2003, NATO assumed command of

ISAF and this gave further legitimacy to the war.

The war with the Taliban insurgents in Afghanistan continues to this day and President Barrack Obama has committed to increased troops to Afghanistan to help maintain peace and security.

The Iraq War: in contrast to the Gulf War, the Iraq War was a US-led invasion (there were troops from a number of US allies in the coalition force but it was predominantly based on US military and resources and regime-change efforts outside the collective security arrangement of the UN Security Council), based on the new Bush Doctrine. Following allegations that Iraq possessed weapons of mass destruction (WMD) and supported Al Qaeda, the US President, George W. Bush, launched *Operation Iraqi Freedom,* with approval from the US Senate and Congress, based on the Constitution of the US and US law. Citing the Iraq Liberation Act of 1998, the resolution reiterated that it was the policy of the US to remove the Hussein regime and promote a democratic government in Iraq.

A number of US allies were opposed to the war, including France, Germany and Canada. There were serious legal questions surrounding the launching of the war and the UN Secretary General, Kofi Annan, said of the invasion, "I have indicated it was not in conformity with the UN Charter. From our point of view, from the Charter point of view, it was illegal." The Bush Administration's rationale for the Iraq War has faced a lot of criticism from both inside and outside the US, with many US citizens finding parallels with the Vietnam War. The turmoil in Iraq continues to this day and while much progress has been made in installing a democratic government and in reducing troop and civilian causalities, there is still a long way to go before Iraq can be considered a stable, peaceful and independent country once again. The cost of the war has been huge for the US and estimates put the direct cost of the war at more than $700 Billion and total indirect costs at more than $3 Trillion.

Failure of the UN to Prevent Internal Conflict & Genocide: one area where the UN and its Charter for collective security has failed miserably, has been in the prevention of genocide, ethnic cleansing and other internal crises and crimes against humanity, in failed or authoritarian states. The very founding of the UN, as outlined in Article 1, was to maintain international peace and security.

Some members of the UNSC have interpreted this in the strictest sense, arguing that internal conflicts do not pose a threat to international security, hence cannot be resolved under the UN Charter. Article 2 also guarantees sovereign equality and prevents the UN from intervening in matters within the domestic jurisdiction of any State which has been invoked, to prevent action against States that commit crimes of humanity on their own people. A number of internal crises and crimes against humanity have been committed over the years without any or little response from the international community and the UN, including civil wars and genocide campaigns in Angola, Iraq, Yugoslavia, Rwanda, Sri Lanka, Kosovo, Burma, Darfur and other developing countries.

A few exceptions of international involvement include NATO's involvement in Bosnia and Kosovo, which it did without the backing of the UN Security Council, and India's intervention in the crisis in Sri Lanka, without much success. Hundreds of thousands of people have been killed, mutilated, raped and robbed by their own States and governments without any support or collective security from the international community. Following the genocide in Rwanda and the UN and international community's failure to intervene, the then Secretary General, Kofi Annan, raised several questions, including the responsibility of the international community to protect civilian populations against their own governments.

The International Commission on Intervention and State Sovereignty (ICISS), released its first report in December 2001, and the concept of 'Responsibility to Protect' was born. The report discussed the critical question of when State sovereignty should yield to protection against crimes and violations of humanitarian law and the responsibility of the international community in preventing them. At the 2005 UN World Summit, member States included 'Responsibility to Protect' in the Outcome Document, with countries such as Argentina, Chile, Mexico, Rwanda and South Africa taking a leadership role in the discussions. Paragraphs 138-139 of the World Summit Outcome Document outline the 'Responsibility to Protect Agreement' which include the following:

- That each individual State has the primary responsibility to protect its populations from genocide, war crimes, crimes against humanity and ethnic cleansing. And it is also a responsibility for prevention of these crimes.
- That the international community should encourage or assist States to exercise this responsibility.
- The international community has the responsibility to use appropriate diplomatic, humanitarian and other peaceful means to help protect populations threatened by these crimes. When a State manifestly fails in its protection responsibilities, and

peaceful means are inadequate, the international community must take stronger measures, including collective use of force authorized by the Security Council under Chapter VII.

In 2006, the UN Security Council adopted Resolution 1674, which formalized the UNSC support for the norm. The Security Council also passed Resolution 1706, authorizing deployment of UN peacekeeping troops in Darfur, which was the first action of the UNSC based on the 'Responsibility to Protect Agreement'. The UN General Assembly also passed Resolution A/RES/63/308, in September 2009, and 'Responsibility to Protect' was adopted by UNGA[34]. The actual implementation has had some setbacks, including the failure of the international community to act in Myanmar, but steady progress is being made towards the day when the International community and the UN will be bound to protect people from crimes committed by their own governments.

Despite its failures, the UNSC remains the best and only means for world peace. The UNSC and the General Assembly continue to discuss and pass resolutions on various issues but one has to keep in mind that the support of the US for these resolutions is very important in today's world order. As the sole super power and the most dominant country in the world and given that no other power is willing or capable of leading action in support of UNSC resolutions, US leadership for collective security is of paramount importance. Growing powers such as the EU, China, Brazil and India, must demonstrate leadership and their ability and willingness to take the lead in negotiating and implementing UN resolutions.

---

34 http://www.responsibilitytoprotect.org/index.php/about-rtop

Many nations have called for UN reforms, particularly in relation to the most important and powerful organ of the UN, the Security Council. But they have not shown leadership in tackling global issues or ability to maintain collective security. With the US military actively engaged in two different conflicts simultaneously in Afghanistan and Iraq and the economy going through a recession, the emotional and economic tolls of these actions are showing on the super power. Now is the time and the opportunity for emerging leaders like India, with growing economies and substantial reserves, to step up to the leadership role and to show their capabilities and willingness in maintaining collective global security.

INDIA & THE UNITED NATIONS

India attained her freedom two years after the end of the Second World War and the formation of the UN. Jawaharlal Nehru, India's first Prime Minister, had an idealistic view of and great expectations from, the UN. In a broadcast titled 'An Age of Crises'[35], made to the USA from New Delhi, in April 1948, he expressed his vision and ideal of *Vasudhaiva Kutumbakam* as a role for the UN, wherein it would become for nations what nations were for individuals – a world government under which all nations could prosper. Excerpts from the broadcast include:

"We talk of World Government and One World and millions yearn for it. Earnest efforts continue to be made to realize this ideal of the human race which has become so imperative today."

---

35 Jawaharlal Nehru, India's Foreign Policy: Selected Speeches, September 1946-April 1961 – Publications Division Indian Ministry of Information and Broadcasting, 1961.

"I have no doubt in my mind that World Government must and will come…"

"The machinery for it is not difficult to device. It can be an extension of the federal principle, a growth of the idea underlying the United Nations, giving each national unit freedom to fashion its destiny according to its genius, but subject always to the basic covenant of the World Government."

Nehru's idealism was rocked by the UN's handling of the Kashmir issue during the First Indo-Pakistan War of 1947-48. To the dismay of Nehru and his government, the issue got embroiled in the politics of the Cold War and most discussions at the UN were partisan in nature. He became increasingly disillusioned about the resolution of India's bilateral territorial disputes through the UN and in October 1950, when China ignited a serious political situation in Tibet, India showed little enthusiasm for the issue at the UN, preferring to rely on bilateral relationships and talks. In a speech delivered at the Indian Council of World Affairs, Constitution Club in 1949, and titled, 'Our Foreign Policy'[36], he stated: "The United Nations Organization has most of the nations of the world in it, but it is true that it is dominated more or less by certain great nations of Europe and America, with the result that the main problems discussed there are the problems of Europe and America."

The First Kashmir War, 1947-48: the Indo-Pakistan War of 1947, or the First Kashmir War, started when the Azad Kashmir forces, comprising of troops from the Pakistan army, paramilitary and local militias of the North West

---

36 *Independence and after*: a collection of speeches by Jawaharlal Nehru, 1946-1949.

Frontier Province, invaded the princely state of Jammu and Kashmir. The Maharaja of Jammu and Kashmir asked for Indian military assistance and agreed to accede to India. The Government of India recognized the accession as the new Indian state of Jammu and Kashmir and sent Indian troops to defend it against the Azad Kashmir forces. Indian forces were successful in repelling the attack and drove the Azad Kashmir forces out of the major cities in Jammu and Kashmir.

After Indian forces gained the upper hand in most sectors and had pursued the Azad Kashmir forces as far as Kargil, Prime Minister Jawaharlal Nehru, decided to ask the UN to intervene. A UN ceasefire was arranged for on 31st December 1948, and the terms were laid out in the UNCIP (UN Commission for India and Pakistan) Resolution of 13 August. The terms included: Pakistan to withdraw its forces, both regular and irregular while allowing India to maintain minimum strength of its forces to preserve law and order and to conduct a plebiscite to determine the future of the territory. There was a withdrawal of forces and both governments accepted the crease-file line in July 1949.

Following this, they could not agree on the details of a plebiscite for a permanent settlement of the problem. In March 1950, the UNSC terminated the UNCIP and established a UN representative to mediate. In 1949, the UN also established the UN Military Observer Group in India and Pakistan (UNMOGIP), to supervise the cease-fire which continues to report violations of the cease-fire line to the UN Secretary General, to this day[37].

---

37 http://www.un.org/en/peacekeeping/missions/unmogip/index.shtml

The Second Indo-Pakistan War: emboldened by India's loss to China in the Sino-Indian War in 1962, Pakistan launched *Operation Gibraltar* in August 1965 – with the goal of infiltrating forces into Jammu and Kashmir to precipitate an insurgency against India. Pakistani soldiers crossed the Line of Control and were engaged by Indian forces, tipped off by the local populace. India then crossed the international border on the western front, marking the official beginning of the war. The Indian army soon marched within range of the Lahore International Airport. An important point to keep in mind is that most of the weapons of the Pakistan Air Force and Army were US-made, while the Indian Air Force flew an assortment of Russian and European aircraft. The US supplied weapons and technology to Pakistan to fight Communism but these were employed by Pakistan in their war against India.

Dismayed, the US imposed an embargo against further supplies once the war started, which affected Pakistan since the majority of their equipment was American made. Pakistan's hope and strategy was for a quick win as they believed they had superior weapons. But their plans were dashed when India opened a new frontier in the war. India had more resources to fight a wider and a more prolonged war and by expanding the theatre of war, India took away the weapons advantage that Pakistan had. By the time the war ended in September 1965, most neutral observers noted that Indian forces had won decisively and could have even marched on into Pakistani territory.

On 20 September, the UNSC unanimously passed Resolution 211[38], which called for an unconditional ceasefire

---

38   http://daccess-dds-ny.un.org/doc/RESOLUTION/GEN/NR0/222/82/IMG/ NR022282.pdf?OpenElement

from both nations – to take effect on Wednesday, 22 September 1965, at 0700 GMT – and for both governments to withdraw all armed personnel to the positions held by them before 5 August 1965. The Soviet Union, led by Premier Alexey Kosygin, hosted ceasefire negotiations in Tashkent, in January 1966 – where Indian Prime Minister, Lal Bahadur Shastri, and Pakistani President, Ayub Khan, signed the Tashkent Declaration[39]. The Declaration was a framework for co-operation that included Indian and Pakistani troops going back to their pre-conflict positions; non-interference in each other's internal affairs; and restoration of diplomatic and economic relations. This declaration remained till the Third Indo-Pakistan War in 1971.

The Third Indo-Pakistan War & the Formation of Bangladesh: the Third Indo-Pakistan War was a singular triumph for India and resulted in the break-up of Pakistan (East & West), into Bangladesh and Pakistan. This break-up resulted in loss of land, resources, army and pride for Pakistan. The official war started on 3 December 1971, when Pakistan launched a pre-emptive strike on 11 Indian airbases and it lasted just 13 days. Days after the war erupted, the matter was discussed at the UNSC and Resolution 303[40] was adopted, which noted the lack of unanimity of its permanent members at the meetings of the UNSC, leading to its inability to exercise its primary responsibility for the maintenance of international peace and security (the Soviet Union which supported India and the formation of Bangladesh, vetoed any UNSC action), and referred the question to the General Assembly. The impact of the Cold War on the activities of the UN could be clearly seen in this conflict as well.

---

39 http://www.stimson.org/southasia/?SN=SA20020116299
40 http://daccess-dds-ny.un.org/doc/RESOLUTION/GEN/NR0/261/63/IMG/NR026163.pdf?OpenElement

In the days and weeks leading up to the war, there were numerous reports of genocide and atrocities being committed by the Pakistani army and approximately 10 million refugees fled East Pakistan, taking refuge in neighboring Indian states. General Tikka Khan earned the nickname of 'Butcher of Bengal', due to the widespread atrocities he committed. The Nixon administration in the US ignored the reports it received of these activities and continued to support Pakistan based on the fear that the defeat of Pakistan would mean total Soviet domination of the area. Instead of collective support against genocide and for the right of self-determination of the people of East Pakistan, the UNSC discussions were along the partisan lines of the West and Communist blocs. The Indian Army joined forces with the Mukti Bahini, to form the Mitro Bahini, and employed a swift three-pronged assault that rapidly converged on Dhaka. Pakistani forces surrendered on 16 December 1971, when the Instrument of Surrender was signed by the Commander of Pakistani forces in East Pakistan and the General Office Commanding-in-Chief, Eastern Command, of the Indian Army.

The Simla Agreement between India and Pakistan cemented the status of the new nation of Bangladesh, and secured the release of over 90,000 prisoners-of-war held by India. It laid down a framework for co-operation between the two nations. However, the agreement failed to clearly define the border in the Siachen Glacier-Saltoro Ridge area and the result was the Siachen War in 1984, during which, India successfully established control over all of the 70km-long Siachen Glacier and the three main passes of the Saltoro Ridge west of the glacier.

The Fourth Indo-Pakistan War or the Kargil War: in the war between India and Pakistan post-9/11, and in a world where threats to global security came primarily from terrorism-related activities, the world was united in its condemnation of Pakistan's role. Pakistan, though an ally of the US in the war on terrorism, is one the breeding grounds for terrorists and has lost much international sympathy and support due to its failure to close down *madarassas* or religious schools, some of which promote an extreme view of Islam and *jihad* against the non-Islam world. The war broke out when Pakistani soldiers and Kashmiri militants infiltrated into positions on the Indian side of the Line of Control (LOC) and seized unoccupied (for the winter), Indian military posts. The Indian Army, along with the Air Force, recaptured a majority of the positions on the Indian side and international diplomatic pressure forced Pakistan to withdraw from the few remaining Indian positions. Though the UNSC did not pass any resolutions on this conflict, there was substantial international support for India and condemnation of Pakistan's actions. Relations between India and Pakistan continue to be frosty.

The Sino-India War: this war marked a turning point in India's foreign policy and strategy and a change in philosophy towards external affairs, from one based on Idealism to one based on realism. Nehru's vision of *Hindi-Chini Bhai-Bhai* and his foreign policy based on the *Panchsheel,* was turned upside down when China invaded India in 1962. India was ill-prepared for the assault and suffered a quick defeat at the hands of the Chinese. This conflict also highlighted the inability of the UNSC to provide for collective security as it was embroiled in the Cuban Missile Crisis of the Cold War, which happened at the same time.

The US and Soviet Union were at a stand-off and the Cuban Missile Crisis was probably the closest the world has got to a Third World War, involving both the super powers of the time. Cold War politics and the intensity of the Cuban Missile Crisis, meant that India got no support from the collective security arrangement of the UN and this prompted the first real change in policy that led to the build-up of India's defense forces. India came to accept the importance of defense preparedness and the use of force in international politics and embarked on a substantial program of military modernization. It committed itself to the creation of a million-strong army with ten new mountain divisions equipped and trained for high altitude warfare, a 45-squadron air force with supersonic aircraft, and a modest program of naval expansion. This attitudinal and strategic shift would help India defeat Pakistan in the wars of 1965 and 1971.

India and the Non-Aligned Movement: the Non-Aligned Movement is one of Nehru's (along with the President of Egypt, Gamal Abdul Nasser; Ahmed Suharno of Indonesia; Kwame Nkrumah of Ghana; and Yugoslav President, Josip Broz Tito), singular contributions to modern world politics and is a cornerstone of India's foreign policy. The beginning of the Cold War coincided with India gaining her independence in 1947. Having emerged from colonial rule after 200 years, Indian leaders and the general populace were in no mood to be led again by either of the power blocs of the Cold War. Nehru and other post-independence policymakers, were keen to maintain national autonomy in external affairs and explicitly sought to forge a pathway that would keep India outside the ambit of the Cold War. Thus the non-alignment strategy was born.

A number of other newly independent countries in Asia and Africa, shared these sentiments and held a conference in Bandung, Indonesia, in 1955, where they adopted the 'Ten Principles of Bandung'[41]. These included:

1. Respect of fundamental human rights and of the objectives and principles of the Charter of the United Nations.
2. Respect of the sovereignty and territorial integrity of all nations.
3. Recognition of the equality among all races and of the equality among all nations, both large and small.
4. Non-intervention or non-interference into the internal affairs of another -country.
5. Respect of the right of every nation to defend itself, either individually or collectively, in conformity with the Charter of the United Nations.
6. A. Non-use of collective defense pacts to benefit the specific interests of any of the great powers. B. Non-use of pressures by any country against other countries.
7. Refraining from carrying out or threatening to carry out aggression, or from using force against the territorial integrity or political independence of any country.
8. Peaceful solution of all international conflicts in conformity with the Charter of the United Nations.
9. Promotion of mutual interests and of cooperation.
10. Respect of justice and of international obligations.

---

41 http://www.namegypt.org/en/AboutName/HistoryAndEvolution/Pages/default.aspx

Six-years later, the Non-Aligned Movement (NAM), was officially founded at the First Summit Conference at Belgrade. The primary objectives of the non-aligned countries focused support for self-determination and territorial integrity of States, as well as opposition to apartheid, imperialism, colonialism, neo-colonialism and racism. The members of NAM were also opposed to all forms of foreign aggression, occupation, domination, interference or hegemony, as well as against great power bloc politics. The non-aligned nations are independent countries that chose not join any of the Cold War blocs. NAM played a significant role in the UN General Assembly and other political fora, in the decolonization of a number of African countries and NAM members were staunchly opposed to apartheid in South Africa.

In the mid-70s, the Algeria summit came out with a demand for a new world economic order to counter the under-development in the majority of countries in Africa, Asia and Latin America.

The NAM also had many setbacks. It was ineffective and could not resolve or intervene when member countries were involved in war. Examples include the wars between India and Pakistan and the Iran-Iraq conflict between1980 and 1988.

India's commitment to NAM was questioned when India and the Soviet Union signed the Indo-Soviet Treaty of Peace, Friendship and Cooperation in 1971, prior to the Indo-Pakistan War in the same year. Nevertheless, NAM continued to play an important role in world politics until the break-up of the Soviet Union. The end of the Cold War meant that some of the basic premises of the founding of

NAM were no longer there. The movement had to realign its objectives with the changing nature of the world structure and began to focus on economic issues.

NAM provides a platform for developing countries that are under-represented in the policy and decision-making bodies of the UN. Almost 20 years have passed since the end of the Cold War but problems of poverty and exploitation, as well as under-development, continue to plague developing nations. NAM continues to provide a platform for developing countries to act together to solve some of their most pressing and difficult problems. NAM is also an outspoken critic of US actions on the international stage – specifically post-9/11, where the US unilaterally invaded Iraq with the aim of regime change. India has a chance once again to revitalize and make NAM a relevant and purposeful organization, just as Nehru made a deep contribution to its founding. India must demonstrate its leadership in NAM by reviving its relevance as a platform to lead the restructuring of the current world system by democratizing the UN and its various policy-making organs.

Reforms are needed to improve the operations and transparency, as well as the broader representation, of these policy-making bodies. One must remember that the UN was founded on the Atlantic Charter, which was a coalition of the Allies in the Second World War – an alliance created by the US for the purpose of winning a war – thus the US and its close allies have disproportionate power in the policy- making bodies of the UN. If the UN is to be truly representative of the people of the world,and as Nehru envisioned, a World Government, the Non-Aligned Movement must continue to position itself against the indifference and opposition from the masters of the present system. India must play a significant role in this resurgence of NAM.

India's Role in UN Peace-keeping Missions: India the second largest troop-contributor countries to the UN, and more than 100,000[42] Indian personnel have participated in 35 UN peacekeeping missions around the world. Indian troops have taken part in some of the most difficult operations and suffered casualties in the service of the UN. India has demonstrated its unique capacity to sustainin large troop commitments over prolonged periods.

Among the success stories of UN operations, is Namibia. Indian military observers in Namibia were responsible for the smooth withdrawal of foreign troops, elections and the subsequent handing over of authority to the new government. Indian personnel, as part of UN peacekeeping missions, have contributed significantly in many conflicts and post-war efforts around the world, including Vietnam; as the Chairman of the Neutral Nations Repatriation Commission in Korea; as part of the United Nations Emergency Force(UNEF) in the Middle East; as part of the UN Operation ONUC in the Congo; as part of the UN Observer Mission in Yemen; as part of the UN Iraq-Kuwait Observer Mission (UNIKOM) after the Gulf War; and in various other locations. This level of support for UN missions has helped propel India into a leadership role on the world stage. India must continue this policy to attain its broader goal of making a significant impact on the world stage.

---

42 Statement by External Affairs Minister, Mr. S.M. Krishna, at the general debate during the 64th session of the UN General Assembly, http://www.indianembassy.org/page.php?id=457

IPKF: though the Indian Peace Keeping Force (IPKF) mission in Sri Lanka was not UN mandated, nor was it entirely successful, it is important to understand what happened in order to appreciate the responsibilities and the perils of a regional power. Some have compared India's experience in Sri Lanka to that of America's experience in Vietnam, but there are fundamental differences between these operations.

The Vietnam War was driven by the Cold War ideology (the US had no historical relationship or otherwise with the people of Vietnam), while the IPKF mission was driven by a combination of history, ethnic connections (the Tamils in Sri Lanka are of Indian descent), domestic political pressure (sympathy for the Tamil cause in the state of Tamil Nadu), and India's ambition to be a regional power. India sent a contingent of its military to Sri Lanka to perform a peace-keeping role under the mandate of the Indo-Sri Lanka Accord of 1987 (signed between Indian Prime Minister, Rajiv Gandhi and Sri Lankan President, J.R. Jayewardene), to help resolve the civil war in the Island nation.

The main task of the IPKF was to disarm the different militant groups including the Liberation Tigers of Tamil Eelam (LTTE) and help in the formation of an Interim Administrative Council (similar to many peace-keeping missions around the world authorized by the UNSC). The mission soon got embroiled in battle with the LTTE, which refused to disarm and tried to dominate the Interim Administrative Council. The IPKF was involved in several combat operations over two years, in which, a number of LTTE guerillas, civilians, as well as over 1000 IPKF personnel, were killed.

A combination of circumstances – change of governments in both India (Vishwanath Pratap Singh was elected Prime Minister) and Sri Lanka (Ranasinghe Premadasa was the elected Sri Lankan President), and strong public opinion in Sri Lanka against the operation, led India to withdraw the IPKF. The last contingents left in March 1990. Many neutral organizations alleged that both the IPKF and the LTTE engaged in battle with scant regard for civilian safety and they violated human rights. Indian forces were accused of a number of human rights violations including civilian massacres in the north-eastern province of Sri Lanka (Valvettiturai massacre; Jaffna teaching hospital massacre etc), highlighting the challenges of ensuring proper conduct of peace-keeping forces. The LTTE employed a suicide mission and assassinated Rajiv Gandhi in 1991, for his role in sending the IPKF to Sri Lanka. Norway helped mediate a cease fire in 2002, but sporadic incidents of violence continued until the LTTE began a more aggressive campaign in late-2005, followed by the Sri Lankan offensive in 2006.

In January 2008, the Sri Lankan government officially pulled out of the cease fire agreement and a fullscale operation against the LTTE was launched. Vellupillai Prabhakaran, the leader of the LTTE, was killed and in May 2009, the war was declared over. India's experience in this conflict was mixed and while India tried to act as a responsible regional power, it was not successful in its mission. Should India have involved a larger coalition or a UN mandated implementation of the accord? Should India have raised the issue at the UN or UNSC? Should India have involved the LTTE at the original Indo-Sri Lanka Accord of 1987? Should India have stayed longer to complete the mission? What would India do today if it faced a similar situation? These are important questions to consider and answer as India seeks to have a larger influence in the world, with a seat at the UN Security Council. No situations are more important for India to demonstrate its leadership abilities than those in its immediate region.

Though India provided substantial humanitarian relief[43] to the camps set up for internally displaced people (of Tamil origin), when the conflict intensified in 2008 and 2009, many have criticized India's lack of political involvement and capacity to influence events in the later stages of Sri Lanka's operations against the LTTE, accusing the Sri Lankan army of crimes against the Tamil people. For a country that aspires to be a custodian of international peace as a member of the UN Security Council, this inability to influence events in its region reflects poorly on India's capacity to be an effective member of the UNSC.

India's Role in World Events & Foreign Policy Post the Cold War: subsequent to India's pullout from Sri Lanka in 1990, major global changes have restructured geo-politics, including the collapse of the erstwhile Soviet Union and the end of the Cold War in 1991. Iraq invaded Kuwait in 1990, leading to the UN-sanctioned Persian Gulf War, and India faced a major balance of payments crisis in 1991, when the government came close to default. India's foreign exchange reserves had dwindled to a point where India could barely finance three weeks worth of imports (primarily petrol), and had to airlift gold to the Bank of England as collateral. India engaged with the IMF and initiated a series of economic reforms that helped India lift itself out of the economic doldrums and begin its journey to a strong financial future.[44]

---

43 Ministry of External Affairs of India, http://meaindia.nic.in/, Press releases 2008
44 More on this topic in the next chapter — India's role in the monetary and financial world

Globalization and the emergence of transnational corporations, heralded changes in the business environment. This was also a period of American dominance, a time when the US was and continues to be, the sole super power in the world; and the emergence of terrorist threats to the US and other countries in Europe. The 9/11 attacks and subsequent 'Bush Doctrine' of American unilateralism, as well as its wars in Afghanistan and Iraq, dominated headlines. India was also rocked by communal violence in the aftermath of the destruction of the Babri Masjid in Ayodhya, in 1992, and numerous terrorist attacks since then have caused loss of life, peace, security and property.

During these tumultuous years, India was mostly inwardly focused on developing its economy and furthering reforms as well as tackling rising communal and terrorist threats. There are, however, a few important developments that need to be reviewed in the years since the Cold War.

1. India's growing ties in Asia and the Look East policy
2. India's nuclear explosions in 1998 and its assertion of nuclear capabilities
3. India's growing relationship with the US
4. The signing of the Civilian Nuclear cooperation agreement
5. The rising threat of terrorism.

Look East Policy: a significant foreign policy of these times was the Look East Policy where India began focusing on developing stronger relationships with countries in its immediate geography. India's relationship with China is a key component of the Look East Policy. Despite border issues between India and China, trade between the countries continues to grow rapidly. It reached over $50 Billion in 2008, and there is a developing bilateral relationship between the two nations. The Look East Policy was also a way for India to bridge the 'historical deficiency' that Mr. Pranab Mukherjee referred to in his speech at the Carnegie Endowment in 2005[45]. One of the outcomes of this policy has been the change in India's attitude and relationship with Myanmar (Burma).

India had traditionally supported Burma's pro-democracy movement but in 1993, reversed its policy and signed trade and investment agreements with the military junta. India also signed free trade agreements with many East Asian economies, including a comprehensive economic co-operation agreement with Singapore. India became a summit level partner on par with China, Japan and Korea in ASEAN (Association of South East Asian Nations) in 1996, and the first India-ASEAN business summit was held in New Delhi in 2002.

India's Nuclear Explosions (1998) & Assertion of her Nuclear Capabilities: in 1998, India conducted five underground nuclear tests in Pokhran, taking the world by surprise. Two weeks later, Pakistan responded with its own nuclear weapons tests. Both countries in the sub-continent were now nations with declared nuclear weapons, though neither had signed the Non-Proliferation Treaty (NPT). The tests invited sanctions from the US and other major world powers. The UN Security Council adopted Resolution 1172, condemning the tests by both countries and demanded they refrain from further tests. India's demonstration of its nuclear weapons showed the complete shift in its strategy in foreign relations towards

---

45 www.carnegieendowment.org/files/Mukherjee_Transcript_06-27-051.pdf

realism. The sanctions imposed by the US and other nations, were soon lifted and in 2000, President Bill Clinton visited India and had bilateral and economic discussions with India's Prime Minister, A.B. Vajpayee.

India-US Relationship: liberalization of the economy in India and the growing economic and trade links with the US, as well as the realization of common characteristics, values and interests, led to a significant improvement in relations between the world's two foremost democracies. China's growing influence in Asia and around the world, might also have played a part in the growing relationship between the US and India – part of America's strategy to counter China, referred to as 'containment'. Common concerns over extremism and terrorism, as well as energy, security, and climate change, have helped bolster relations between the two nations. In 2004, the US and India launched the Next Steps in Strategic Partnership (NSSP), which led to the transformation of bilateral relationships.

In July 2007, the US and India reached a historic milestone by completing the negotiations on the agreement for peaceful nuclear co-operation, also known as the 123 Agreement – which allowed American and Indian firms to participate in each other's civil nuclear energy sectors. In exchange, India agreed to separate its civil and military nuclear facilities and place all its civil nuclear facilities under International Atomic Energy Agency (IAEA) safeguards. To complete the agreement, a number of steps, including an amendment of US domestic law, an India-IAEA agreement, and an exemption from the Nuclear Suppliers Group, in addition to ratification by both the US and Indian legislatures, was required.

The NSG waiver makes India the only known country with nuclear weapons, which is not a party to the NPT but is still allowed to carry out nuclear commerce with the rest of the world. On 8 October 2008, President Bush signed into law, the United States-India Nuclear Cooperation Approval and Non-Proliferation Enhancement Act.

On 9 July 9 2008, India formally submitted the safeguards agreement to the IAEA, and the Indian government after surviving a no-confidence motion, signed the 123 Agreement with the US on 10 October, 2008, making it fully operational. This agreement signals the growing strategic importance of India to the US, as well as an acknowledgement of India's growing power in the region – a clear victory for the realist perspective strategists.

The Rising Threat of Terrorism: India has been rocked by a numerous terrorist attacks, most of which have been traced back to Pakistan. The insurgency in Jammu and Kashmir is also known to be supported by the Pakistani Intelligence Agency ISI (Inter-Services Intelligence). The most daring of these was the attack on the Indian Parliament in New Delhi on 13 December 2001. Five terrorists were involved in the operation and entered the Parliament compound in a car through the VIP gate. They set off massive blasts and fought a 45 minute battle with Indian security forces. All five terrorists, later identified as Pakistani nationals, were killed in the battle.

Mumbai (Bombay), the financial capital of India, also witnessed a number of terrorist attacks. A series of 30 bombs in various locations, killing 257 people in 1993, were attributed to Dawood Ibrahim and his mafia D-company. A number of bomb explosions in 2003, at various locations including car bombs near the Gateway of India and Zaveri

Bazaar, killed 50 people. A series of seven bombs in local trains, killing 209, were traced to Lashkar-e-Taiba and the Students Islamic Movement of India. The coordinated Mumbai attack in 2008 that included attacks at the Taj Mahal Hotel, Chabad House and Leopold Café, were traced back to Lashkar-e-Taiba, as were the bomb explosions at the German Bakery in Pune (close to Mumbai), killing 14 people.

A number of Indian cities have been the targets of terrorism, including New Delhi, Mumbai, Bangalore, Ahmedabad, Ludhiana, Lucknow, Varanasi, Faizabad, Hyderabad, Malegaon and Jaipur – in addition to the almost continuous outbreaks of violence in Jammu and Kashmir. The north-eastern region of India has also experienced increased terrorist activity with bomb blasts in Agartala, Imphal and Guwahati in 2008 and Guwahati again in 2009.

India's response to terrorism has been a blend of using hard and soft power. India used diplomatic pressure on Pakistan to try to delink the ISI-terrorist links, as well as to engage Pakistan in a dialogue on resolving the issue, while strengthening its intelligence and police capabilities. The government also enacted the Prevention of Terrorist Activities Act (POTA) in 2002, which was later replaced by the Unlawful Activities (Prevention) Act in 2004 –strengthened in 2008, giving greater authority to law enforcement agencies to detain and question suspects (some human rights activists have called these Acts draconian and claim law enforcement agencies have misused them and perpetrated human rights violations). Border security, as well as security measures at airports and other targets of high importance, have been increased.

Terrorism remains one of India's biggest threats to peace

and prosperity. Sharing borders with Pakistan and Bangladesh, as well as being close to Afghanistan, puts India right in the middle of one of the most unstable regions of the world.

The UN Security Council has taken a number of steps to deal with terrorism. Resolution 1267 created a sanctions committee that maintains a list of individuals and entities related to the Taliban, Osama-bin-Laden and Al Qaeda. The resolution requires all countries to identify and freeze any assets and prevent the transit of people and supply of arms, to those identified on the list. The UNSC, through Resolution 1373, established the Counter-Terrorism Committee (described by the then Secretary General Kofi Annan, as the center of global efforts to fight terrorism), with the mandate of assisting member States to comply with terrorism- related conventions and protocols. It later created a stronger center, the Counter Terrorism Executive Directorate (CTED), with more resources allocated through Resolution 1535 in 2004. The General Assembly adopted resolution 62/272[46] in 2008, affirming the global community's commitment to counter terrorism.

A number of countries also entered into bilateral agreements to share intelligence and resources in the fight against terrorism. India and the US signed a counter terrorism initiative in 2010, that included freezing assets and financial flows to terrorist networks. They agreed to increase co-operation and intelligence sharing, as well as joint probes in bomb blasts, creating a bilateral strategic partnership in the fight against terrorism.

---

46 http://daccess-dds-ny.un.org/doc/UNDOC/GEN/N07/480/03/PDF/N0748003. pdf? OpenElement

UNITED NATIONS REFORMS

There have been calls for reforming the UN, ever since its founding. Many debates revolve on the role the UN should play in world affairs, with some advocating a greater and more effective role (similar to a World Government), while others wanting it to play a more subdued humanitarian role (arguably the role it plays today). There are also two other perspectives on reforming the operations of the UN:

1. the developed nations who contribute a majority of the money and resources that finance UN operations, want administrative reform to improve efficiencies;

2. the developing nations who want greater representation at the Institution and more democratic conduct of UN operations.

The developed nations have consistently prevailed in their agenda as they control the finances of the organization and have, at times, resorted to withholding their assessment payments (such as the US withholding payments to the UN under the Reagan administration), as a means of achieving their goals.

Some have called the years between the late 1950s to the early 1970s, the golden era of the UN – when new institutions such as the UNDP, UNCTAD and UNEP, were created to enhance and enable the UN system to deal with emerging global issues adequately and systematically[47]. This was also a period when important ideas such as the general

---

47 'Reform of the UN system and India', a chapter by Muchkund Dubey in the book, *Indian foreign Policy Challenges and Opportunities* by Atish Sinha and Madhup Mohta, published by the Foreign Service Institute, New Delhi, 2007.

system of preferences, the commodity fund, compensatory financing, special drawing rights (SDRs) and debt forgiveness, were agreed upon in the UN. Several of these initiatives were then taken up by specialized agencies such as the IMF, World Bank, and later, the World Trade Organization (WTO).

These specialized agencies, created outside of the UN at the Bretton Woods Conference, are dominated by the developed countries, where voting is based on a weighted system that gives them voting rights in proportion to their financial contribution, ensuring they have the most authority and control. Through the reform process of rationalization and efficiency, the Secretariat of the UN was stripped of its capabilities in economic, finance and trade matters.

Subsequently, all economic and trade matters, including development, have been discussed outside of the UN General Assembly and confined to these specialized agencies, which many have argued have been used to propagate the Washington Consensus. The UN General Assembly has been reduced to a debating forum where mostly non-consequential speeches are made, while most of the important decisions are taken at the UN Security Council or in the specialized agencies of the IMF, WB and WTO.

It is in this context that it is important to understand the structure and operations, as well as the impact of these specialized agencies, on India and other developing countries of the world. The speech by Venezuelan President, Hugo Chavez, in 2006, is a good example of the kind of inconsequential speeches made at the General Assembly, in which he called the American President, George Bush, "... the Devil".[48]

---

48 http://www.commondreams.org/views06/0920-22.htm

Initial Reforms: after the process of decolonization gained momentum and a number of new members were admitted into the UN, the imbalance between the number of seats in the UNSC and the total number of member States became stark. The only significant reform of the UNSC came in 1965, when the non-permanent membership of the UNSC was increased from six to ten.

Subsequent Reforms: Kofi Annan, the then Secretary General of the UN, initiated an official reform program in 1997. Reforms on such topics as changing the permanent membership of the Security Council, making the bureaucracy more transparent and accountable, and securing the financial stability of the UN, were proposed[49]. In a report he presented to the General Assembly (51st session, Agenda item 168)[50], he highlighted the following:

- Establishing a new leadership and management structure and decentralization of decision-making.
- Assuring financial solvency through the establishment of a revolving credit fund of up to $1 Billion financed from voluntary contributions.
- Strengthening the Secretariat to serve the UN intergovernmental bodies through the establishment of a consolidated Economic and Social Affairs Group.
- Improving the Organization's ability to deploy peacekeeping and other operations more rapidly and strengthening capacity for post-conflict peace-building.
- Addressing the need for more fundamental change including a thorough review of the UN Charter and the legal instruments from which the specialized agencies of the UN derive their constitutions.

---

49 http://www.un.org/reform/

50 http://daccess-dds-ny.un.org/doc/UNDOC/GEN/N97/189/79/IMG/N9718979.pdf? OpenElement

In 2005, the UN, again under the leadership of Kofi Annan, convened a World Summit, with an agenda to reform the UN. Kofi Annan called the summit, "a once-in-a-generation opportunity to take bold decisions in the areas of development, security, human rights and reform of the United Nations"[51]. Among the key proposals were:

- Expansion of the Security Council to make it more inclusive and representative of the UN's current membership. Two models for expanding the Council from 15 to 24 members were presented: one which envisaged the creation of six new permanent seats and three new non-permanent seats, and the other which recommended the creation of nine new non-permanent seats.
- An enhanced role for the Economic and Social Council.
- Reforms for the procedures of the General Assembly, including rationalization of its agenda to give priority to the most critical issues of the day
- Other proposals for human resource rationalization.

While a number of conclusions from the summit were documented in the World Summit Outcome Document, none of the far-reaching recommendations were implemented. Reforms, as seen by the developed countries, which primarily focused on oversight and efficiency improvements, have been the only ones to see the light of day. Calls for reforming the UN and UNSC membership continue.

Many country leaders have expressed the need

---

51 The 2005 World Summit: An Overview, http://www.un.org/ga/documents/overview2005summit.pdf

for change, such as made by France's President, Nicolas Sarkozy, during a keynote address at Columbia University in March 2010[52]: "Do you young students at Columbia know that not a single African country is a permanent member of the Security Council? [And yet the continent has] a billion inhabitants! Do you know that not a single Arab country [although the Arab world has], about a hundred million inhabitants, is a permanent member of the Security Council? Do you know that India, with a billion inhabitants and becoming the world's most populous nation in 30 years time, is not a permanent member of the Security Council? That Japan, the world's second-largest economy, is not a permanent member of the Security Council? Why? Because 60 years ago they lost the war. Is that reasonable? Do you know that not a single Latin American country is a permanent member of the Security Council? How can anyone expect us to resolve major crises, major wars and major conflicts within the framework of the UN without Africa, without three-quarters of Asia, without Latin America, without a single Arab country? Is that reasonable? Is that sensible? Is it even imaginable? Who can believe that?"

India Demands a Seat at the UNSC

At the UN General Assembly in 1994, India announced its desire/ambition to be part of the UNSC. Since then, support for India's candidature have been slowly growing, with more and more countries supporting India's bid, including Russia, France, UK, Bangladesh, Chile, Croatia and the African Union. The justifications India gives for its bid for a permanent seat are[53]:

- India is the largest democracy in the world, with an

---

52 http://www.un.int/india/2010/ind1702.pdf
53 http://secint04.un.org/india/india_and_the_un_unreform.html

ancient civilization, values and attainments, and a world-view based on universalist inspiration, participative governance, respect for diversity and pluralism, as well as readiness for constructive engagement in the world's affairs. India has been actively involved in the affairs of the United Nations since 1945. It has played an important role in shaping the Cold War and post-Cold War international systems.

- India is one of the leading economies in the world and has the potential to play an increasingly important role in the evolving international economic and financial architecture.

- India's long-standing participation in UN peacekeeping operations testifies not only to the dedication and professionalism of Indian soldiers but also the political will of the government to actively contribute to these operations.

India sought to have a greater say at the UN when Shashi Tharoor, the former Under-Secretary General of the UN, was declared the official candidate of India for the position of UN Secretary-General, after Kofi Annan, in 2006. Tharoor emerged second out of seven contenders in the race.

India Becomes a Non-permanent Member of the UNSC: in October 2010, India was elected as a non-permanent member of the UNSC for a 2-year-term starting in January 2011, with the substantial backing and support of many countries, including Pakistan and China. This was seen by many in India as an opportunity to build trust, confidence and a working relationship with the permanent members of the UNSC, that would bolsters India's quest for permanent membership of the Security Council. The new membership of the Security Council, for the first time, also includes members of all the BRIC countries, giving them an unprecedented opportunity to work together to promote the voice of the developing nations and a majority of the world's population. For the first time, growing middle powers have an opportunity to affect the power structure in the world and begin to transition to a 'balance of power' that will afford them greater say in world affairs.

Events in Libya have challenged this assumption of the ability of BRIC countries to change the current power structure. Despite opposition from all the BRIC countries, who abstained from voting for a UNSC resolution on the No-Fly Zone over Libya, the US and its allies have ratified UNSC Resolution 1973[54], giving the Security Council the authority to use any method necessary, including use of force, to enforce the No-Fly Zone over Libya. Immediately after the ratification, fighter planes from France, and later from Great Britain and the US, began bombing targets in Libya, including the residences of Col. Gaddafi, in what seems to be a repetition of the Western powers actions in Iraq and a definite show of power by them to impose their will in international affairs.

In a response to questions from journalists on why India chose to abstain, the Indian Envoy to the UN, Hardeep Singh Puri, said, "This resolution calls for far-reaching measures but we never got answers to very basic questions. This entire exercise has been based on less than complete information. The UN Special Envoy, who has visited Libya, has not given his report while the African Union is going to send a team to make serious efforts for a peaceful end to the crisis there"[55]. In what seems to be a bureaucratic and

---

54 http://www.un.org/News/Press/docs/2011/sc10200.doc.htm
55 http://ibnlive.in.com/news/india-abstains-from-un-vote-on-libya/146313-3.html

procedural objection rather than one based on principle (the responsibility to protect) or the ability to act swiftly and decisively, India may already be showing its inability to be an effective member of the Security Council or to play a bigger role on the world stage.

FINAL THOUGHTS

Many, including commentators in India, have questioned India's desire for a seat at the UN Security Council and levelled the criticism that in recent years India has not contributed enough to the UN or to international issues to deserve a place at the Security Council. India continues to provide very little financial support to the UN and other specialized bodies under the UN. It has neither put forward any proposals nor vigorously supported any reforms related to financing the UN, to make it financially independent. India has also not shown leadership in international issues, even within its own region, including the humanitarian crisis of civilian Tamils in Sri Lanka in 2009, or advocating 'responsibility to protect' as applied to Myanmar, nor have border issues been resolved with China. Bilateral relations with Pakistan continue to be tenuous and while India has shown immense restraint in its relations with Pakistan, her will or ability to project hard power in addition to soft power in dealing with terrorism emanating from Pakistan, remains doubtful. India faces a number of its own internal security threats and allegations of human rights violations.

Is India really clamoring for a leadership role without the capacity and will to act decisively? India has traditionally been a pacifist country and does not project its military power around the world. India has never initiated a conflict since independence and one does not believe that India will. Does India deserve a seat at the UNSC? If the aim is for democratic representation in the UNSC, then one can argue that India deserves a seat and has rightly justified the reasons – but if the UNSC is to be an effective enforcer of collective security, then it is not enough to be a big democracy or a large economy. India needs to develop its hard power and military capabilities and be ready to use them if necessary. Is India ready to contribute financially, materially and militarily to justify a leadership role at the world body?

The world is looking for concrete steps and actions. India must demonstrate it is ready and capable of such a role. The financial crisis of 2008-09, provided a great opportunity to both India and China to demonstrate their growing power and ability to lead. While the American and European economies suffered severe downturns requiring their governments to spend hundreds of Billions of Dollars to shore them up, the economies in India and China, in contrast, continued to grow respectably. India should have stepped up with increased financial contribution to the UN and its various bodies, demonstrating its growing confidence and ability, as well as bolstering its credentials as a rising power. A great opportunity was wasted.

The current structure of the UN Security Council presents the best opportunity for BRIC countries to make their impact felt and in changing the current power structure. But they must act collectively and decisively. They have already missed the opportunity to affect decision-making at the UNSC on the Libyan crisis by hiding behind procedural and bureaucratic objections. If they do not work together to come out with a co-ordinated action plan to balance power at the UNSC, they might remain spectators to world events.

IMF/WB & India's Place in the World of Money & Finance

3

Humans have traded in goods and services across countries, continents and cultures from time immemorial. The Silk Route, an extensive network of trade routes connecting East, South and Western Asia with the Mediterranean, as well as North Africa and Europe, has been one of the world's oldest and most historically important commercial link trails. Not only were goods exchanged along this route but also religion, customs and philosophies of the day. India, being virtually at the center of the route, played a vital role, trading in spices and precious stones, as well as propagating Buddhism to China and other parts of Asia.

In the beginning people bartered – exchanging goods they made or had for goods and services they needed. With the advent of gold and other commodity money, which had intrinsic value, goods and services could be exchanged or bought by this commodity money. As gold and other precious metals such as silver, had value recognized by everyone, traders were confident about exchanging their goods for these and were sure they could then use the same money to buy other goods that they needed. In contrast, modern trade is based on paper or fiat money. Fiat money does not have any intrinsic value. The value of fiat currency is set by a government in its territory and declared as legal tender though it may not have any value outside that country unless that value is recognized by the government of another country[56].

This raises an important question as to the relative value of fiat money between two countries and how many units of currency one is willing to give for a unit of the other country's currency. An exchange rate, as the term suggests, is the rate one is willing to pay to exchange the money of one country with the legal tender of another[57]. The establishment of a valid and recognized exchange rate is the basis of all international trade and forms a core aspect of international finance. But the key question remains, who sets these exchange rates or how are they determined? How is the value of fiat money or currency of one country compared to that of other countries[58]? And the ultimate question: Can there be one global currency or unit of money that everyone can use to resolve this issue?

---

56 For example a hundred Rupee note has value in India because the government of India guarantees this value, but if the government of Pakistan does not recognize Indian Rupees, this hundred Rupee note will have no value in Pakistan and cannot be used to buy anything there

57 For example, if the government of Pakistan recognizes the Indian Rupee and the exchange rate is set at 2 Pakistani Rupees for every Indian Rupee, then one can convert the hundred Indian Rupees to two hundred Pakistani Rupees and use them to buy goods and services in Pakistan.

58 If Indians want to purchase a number of Pakistan made goods but do not make or have any products that Pakistanis want to buy, then the demand for Pakistani money goes up (need to pay for these goods in Pakistani money), and the exchange rate reflects this demand. Indian Rupees will begin to fetch fewer and fewer Pakistani Rupees and conversely, if Pakistan imports more products from India than it exports to India, the value of the Indian Rupee verses the Pakistani Rupee, will appreciate.

Foreign Exchange Rate Systems

Since the 19th century, there have been three structures or sets of rules regarding foreign exchange rates: the Gold Standard; the Qualified Gold Standard, also known as the Bretton Woods System; and the Flexible Exchange Rate System (either market determined or government regulated and controlled).

The Gold Standard was a system supported by Britain during its hegemonic heyday. The Qualified Gold Standard or the Bretton Woods System, was the standard for the years between the end of the Second World War and 1971, created and supported by the new hegemon in the world – the United States.

The US Dollar became the reserve currency of the world and most other currencies and commodities were priced in dollars. When the US could no longer shoulder the costs of hegemony due to the rising cost of the Vietnam War, as well as large trade deficits, it unilaterally devalued its currency and cancelled the direct convertibility of the US Dollar to gold. This brought the Qualified Gold Standard System to an end. In its place, the current system or the Flexible Exchange Rate System was established – which allowed currencies to float freely and let market forces determine the exchange rate between currencies. Despite the end of US hegemony, the US Dollar continues to be the global reserve currency, with more than 60% of all world trade carried out in US Dollars.

This forces most countries to keep reserves of Dollars to buy goods and services in the international market. This demand for US Dollar denominated foreign reserves and the US Dollar from central banks of countries around the world, allows the US to finance its trade deficit as well as bail itself out of recessions and other economic troubles.

The Gold Standard

The Gold Standard or the Gold Bullion Standard, was a system in which the government of a country guaranteed to sell gold bullion at a fixed price in exchange for their currency. During the years leading to the First World War, the British Pound was the most widely used currency. The British government guaranteed to exchange their currency for gold, which gave the currency value and traders the confidence to accept the British Pound for their goods. Also, as the British government was the most dominant power in the world, no one doubted their ability to exchange their currency for gold. Similarly, most other countries fixed the value of their currency with respect to a weight in gold and this allowed for the determination of exchange rates between different currencies.

Among other things, this led colonial powers to look for gold around the world as the more gold they held, the more money they could circulate in their economy and around the world. Colonial powers also imposed or implemented the Gold Standard in their territories. Britain and other colonial powers imported mostly commodities and agricultural products from their colonies, which were priced very cheap, and exported manufactured goods to their colonies, which were more expensive. This meant that most colonies always suffered from a trade deficit (they had to spend more than they could earn through exports and imports), and often had to borrow Pounds from the British government to pay for the imports. This was another legal way for colonial powers to take gold in exchange for the loans they provided in Pounds to their colonies.

The UK government also acted as the 'lender of last resort' or the bankers' bank. If a country or a central bank in a country ran out of Pounds reserves to pay for imports, they could borrow from Britain. The British government suspended the convertibility of the Pound to gold in 1914, to fund military operations during World War I. By the time the war ended, there was widespread destruction of property and the treasury was depleted by the cost of the war. Britain was no longer the most dominant country in the world and the US was beginning to emerge as the new hegemon – a role it did not accept until the end of the Second World War. This period between the end of the First World War in 1918 and the end of the Second World War in 1945, was a period of great economic turmoil, including the Great Depression that lasted from the stock market crash in 1929, up to the early 1940s.

A Period of Turmoil

The great depression of 1929, which started with the stock market crash of 29 October 1929, also known as Black Tuesday, was the longest, most widespread, and deepest depression of the 20th century. The depression devastated many economies and increased widespread poverty. This was also a period when there was no hegemon to stabilize the world economy. Great Britain was still too weak from the First World War and the US was not ready to take on the mantle of a hegemon to provide the stability needed for the global economy to recover and prosper.

In response, most countries adopted economic nationalist policies and devalued their currency, imposed high import tariffs, and implemented other economic measures such as reducing credit in their economy, to try to climb out of the recession. Currency devaluation is done primarily so that goods from that country become cheaper when exchanged with currencies of other countries. With this move, the country hopes to boost exports and help earn foreign exchange, as well as create domestic employment[59].

When most or all countries, start devaluing their currencies, no one benefits and it has the negative effect of making commodities more expensive, increasing inflation and creating hardship. Import tariffs are raised for exactly the opposite reason. A country raises import tariffs (duties) and it makes the imported item more expensive in the local market, hence it discourages the import of the item. The idea again is to promote domestic manufacturing of the product rather than importing it. So when everyone raised import tariffs, it led to the collapse of international trade.

The most infamous act of raising import tariffs in the US was the Smoot-Hawley Tariff Act of 1930. It raised import tariffs on over 20,000 imported goods to record levels and the ensuing retaliatory tariffs enacted by its partners, reduced American imports and exports by more than 50%. Many economists argue that these US protectionist policies made the depression of 1929 into the great depression and prolonged it. The lessons learnt from the after-effects of these policies led to the dominance of embedded liberal views among the world's economic powers. The beginnings of a new world economic structure

---

59 For eg: if the exchange rate between the Indian Rupee and the Pakistani Rupee is 1:1, then an item made and sold in India for Rs 100 would be priced at 100 Pakistani rupees as well. But if India devalues its currency and announces an exchange of 2 Indian Rupees for every Pakistani Rupee, then Indian businesses can price the same item in Pakistan for 50 Pakistani Rupees, making the item much cheaper than before in Pakistan. This has the effect of destroying local competition and increasing imports of the Item from India, helping Indian domestic manufacturing activity to grow.

were created at the Bretton Woods Conference, when the IMF, WB and GATT, were embedded into the world monetary and economic system.

The Qualified Gold Standard

Towards the end of the Second World War, the US and its allies met at Bretton Woods, New Hampshire, to create a new post-war international monetary and trade system that would help the growth and development of international trade by avoiding the mistakes made during the years of turmoil between the two wars. Economic nationalist ideas such as competitive currency devaluations and raising import tariff barriers, helped none of the developed nations during those years. Keynes and others, argued that co-ordinated action and an embedded liberal policy of economics and trade, would benefit everyone. At this conference, a new body – the International Monetary Fund (IMF), was created, whose primary role was to facilitate a stable and orderly international monetary system and help member countries facing trade deficits and balance of payment difficulties.

Balance of Payments = Current Account + Capital Account
The Current Account is a sum total of imports and exports from a country and remittances by its non-resident citizens. If the value of a country's exports is more than its imports, it will have a Current Account surplus. If the value of imports by a country is more than its exports (+ remittances by citizens living abroad), then it will have a current account deficit.

The Capital Account is a sum total of the value of total foreign investments in stocks, bonds, land and other assets, including foreign direct investment into factories, and the investments made by the country internationally. If the inflow is greater than the outflow, it will have a Capital Account surplus, else it will have a Capital Account deficit.

The US Dollar was now chosen as the reserve currency of the world and its value was fixed with respect to gold. One ounce of gold was set at a value of 35 US Dollars and the US government guaranteed the value of the US Dollar according to this set value. The reason this system is referred to as the Qualified Gold Standard is because all other currencies (other than the US Dollar), could fluctuate against the Dollar depending on market forces. The role of the IMF was to monitor this fluctuation and ensure an orderly setting of exchange rates. All governments at the conference additionally agreed to limit the fluctuation in their currencies to within 1% above or below the par value on any given day.

The IMF became the lender of last resort and countries that had current account deficits or ran into balance of payments issues, could borrow from the IMF to stabilize their currency. This system gave the US a distinct advantage, because the Dollar-gold relationship was fixed, the US could print dollars and spend them freely on a variety of domestic programs such as the Great Society, as well as fund its war in Vietnam. It always had a surplus Capital Account as everyone else needed US Dollars for international trade and bought government bonds. Also, other countries (central banks), were committed to buying up excess dollars in the market to maintain their currency values within the trading bands that they had committed to at the Bretton Woods Conference.

As the US continued to print more and more Dollars

and spend on domestic programs and the war in Vietnam, there was not enough gold reserves to cover all the Dollars circulating in the international system. It also began to run large Current Account deficits. Soon other nations began demanding fulfillment of America's promise to pay. Switzerland redeemed $50 million of paper for gold followed by demands from France, in exchange of $191 million in gold[60]. These redemptions depleted the gold reserves in the US, at which point French President, Charles De Gaulle, complained that France was holding weak Dollars. If France then had decided to redeem all the Dollars it held, it would have emptied the US gold reserves.

Countries began to leave the Bretton Woods system and float their currencies in the open market. West Germany was the first member to leave and soon the value of the Dollar dropped against the Deutsche Mark. Soon Switzerland withdrew the Swiss Franc from the system and it was clear that the Dollar was over-valued.

In 1971 Richard Nixon, the 37th President of the US, unilaterally decided to make dollars non-convertible to gold and imposed a 90-days wage and price freeze, as well as a 10% import surcharge[61]. The US also devalued the Dollar in an effort to close its current Account Deficit. This signalled the end of US hegemony as well as the Qualified Gold Standard period. Soon most currencies were floated in the market (some continue to manage the value of their currency by their central bank operations, also referred to as dirty float, and others to peg their currency to other currencies), and their relative values were determined by

---

60 Frum, David. *How We Got Here, the 70s*, Basic Books, 2000
61 Spero, Joan & Hart, Jeffrey. *The Politics of International Economic Relations*, Wadsworth, Cengage Learning, 2010, 2003

market forces ushering in the current era of the Float or Flexible Exchange Rate System.

THE FLEXIBLE EXCHANGE RATE SYSTEM

At its Jamaica conference in 1976, the Articles of Agreement of the IMF were altered to usher in an era of floating exchange rates. Trading bands were widened so that changes in currency values could more easily reflect the supply and demand of currencies. The rise of OPEC (Organization of Petroleum Exporting Countries), and the dramatic oil price increases in 1973-1974, as well as their demand to be paid in US Dollars, increased the demand for Dollars in the international economy – which helped the Dollar maintain its status as the top currency in the world. As economies around the world continued to grow and the demand for petrol increased, the demand for Dollars continued to rise. Most newly industrialized countries in Asia, including China, began to run huge Current Account surpluses with the US and accumulated vast foreign reserves of the Dollar. The IMF played a central role during the Qualified Gold period and continues to play an important and sometimes controversial role in directing developing economies facing balance of payment crises.

IMF

The International Monetary Fund (IMF), along with the International Bank for Reconstruction & Development, also known now as the World Bank, were created at the Bretton Woods Conference in 1944. The IMF was originally formed to monitor and maintain the Qualified Gold Standard system of exchange rates, primarily between the industrialized countries of Western Europe and the US, and to prevent the rise of economic nationalist policies that were attributed to causing the great depression and subsequently the Second

World War. The task of economic revival of wartorn Europe after the Second World War, was assigned to the WB.

Over the years, the scope of activities of the IMF has increased substantially and in recent times, it is known more for its economic programs in developing countries facing balance of payment crises, than any other of its activities. According to its Articles of Agreement[62], the purposes of the IMF are to promote international monetary cooperation; facilitate the expansion of international trade; promote exchange-rate stability and avoid competitive devaluation; create confidence among member nations; and give them the opportunity to correct balance of payments issues. The IMF was to act as the lender of last resort with short to medium-term funding in order to make the balance of payments disequilibrium shorter and less severe than they would otherwise be. The purposes and articles of agreement embody the liberal perspective of economics.

The IMF came into existence in December 1945, when 29 member countries signed the Articles of Agreement. The IMF's membership began to expand in the late 1950s and the 1960s, as many countries gained their independence from colonial rule. The major exceptions were countries from the Soviet or Communist bloc, many of whom joined only after the end of the Cold War. Today, the IMF has 187 members and is a specialized institution under the UN. The original role of the IMF was envisioned to be like a central bank for central bankers around the world. On joining the IMF, each member had to contribute a certain sum of money, called a quota subscription, as a sort of credit union deposit or chit-fund deposit. The quota was broadly determined by the country's relative size in the world economy.

---

62   http://www.imf.org/external/pubs/ft/aa/aa01.htm

In the IMF system, these quotas have a significant role to play. Firstly, they form a pool of money that the IMF can then lend to member countries facing difficulties and earn interest. Secondly, they are the basis for determining how much each country can borrow from the IMF. Thirdly and most importantly, they determine the voting power of the member. Members who have larger quotas, have a greater say in the operations of the IMF. The US, with the world's largest economy, has the most voting rights of any country, at 16.74% of the total[63]. Quotas are reviewed every five years and can be raised or lowered according to the needs of the IMF and the economic prosperity of the member. Member countries have to pay 25% of the quota in gold or in reserve currencies such as the US Dollar. The remaining 75% can be paid with the member's domestic currency.

The Articles of Agreement also outline the organizational structure of the IMF. They provide for:
1. a Board of Governors (similar to the UN General Assembly), which has representatives from all member countries
2. an Executive Board (similar to the UN Security Council), which is the center of power in the institution and its permanent decision-making body
3. a Managing Director. The Executive Board is composed of 24 directors, of which five are permanent members (US, Japan, Germany, France and the UK).

The other countries are grouped along regional or linguistic lines and send a single representative to the Board. India is grouped with Bangladesh, Bhutan and Sri Lanka and

---

63 http://www.imf.org/external/np/sec/memdir/members.htm

together this group has 2.35% voting rights at the Board[64]. The Fund also has a Managing Director (traditionally it has always been a European), and a staff of experts and civil servants. Major decisions, including change of quotas at the Board, require a 85% super-majority vote. The US has always been the only country able to block a super-majority vote on its own, as it has more than 15% of the vote.

One of the most important Articles of Agreement is Article IV[65], which states each member shall:

- endeavor to direct its economic and financial policies toward the objective of fostering orderly economic growth with reasonable price stability, with due regard to its circumstances;
- seek to promote stability by fostering orderly underlying economic and financial conditions and a monetary system that does not tend to produce erratic disruptions;
- avoid manipulating exchange rates or the international monetary system in order to prevent effective balance of payments adjustment or to gain an unfair competitive advantage over other members;
- follow exchange policies compatible with the undertakings under this section.

Following the collapse of the Qualified Gold Standard and the establishment of the new Flexible Exchange Rate System, the IMF added Surveillance to Article IV:

- The Fund shall oversee the international monetary system in order to ensure its effective

---

64 Voting at the Executive Board http://www.imf.org/external/np/sec/memdir/eds.htm
65 http://www.imf.org/external/pubs/ft/aa/aa04.htm

operation, and shall oversee the compliance of each member with its obligations under Section 1 of this Article.

- In order to fulfill its functions under (a) above, the Fund shall exercise firm surveillance over the exchange rate policies of members, and shall adopt specific principles for the guidance of all members with respect to those policies. Each member shall provide the Fund with the information necessary for such surveillance, and, when requested by the Fund, shall consult with it on the member's exchange rate policies. The principles adopted by the Fund shall be consistent with cooperative arrangements by which members maintain the value of their currencies in relation to the value of the currency or currencies of other members, as well as with other exchange arrangements of a member's choice consistent with the purposes of the Fund and Section 1 of this Article. These principles shall respect the domestic social and political policies of members, and in applying these principles the Fund shall pay due regard to the circumstances of members

This principle in particular has attracted criticism. Opponents say the role of the IMF goes too far in overriding the sovereignty of its member countries as it goes about collecting data and advising member countries on domestic economic policies.

The IMF is a largely self-sustaining organization and the operating budget comes from the one-time contribution or quota that members contribute on joining (they do not physically transfer the money but set it aside at their central banks, as assigned to the IMF), and the interest earned on this as well as other loans the IMF has made to member countries. This gives the IMF a lot of autonomy (as opposed to the UN and its agencies which frequently run into budget problems as they depend on assessments and voluntary contributions). The seven most wealthy nations, referred to as the G7, signed an agreement in 1962, known as the General Agreement to Borrow, allowing the IMF to borrow additional funds from them if it required. They also agreed to never take money from the IMF (they borrow from each other in times of emergency). After a series of crises in the mid-1960s, and a liquidity crisis at the IMF, a new reserve asset called the Special Drawing Right or SDR[66], was created to serve as a unit of exchange at the IMF. Countries with a positive balance of payment purchased SDRs and provided the IMF with additional liquidity, that the IMF used to lend to other members. Members could repay the IMF as well as transact among themselves in SDRs and the value of the SDR is based on a basket of currencies. 1 SDR was equivalent to 1 USD when the Dollar was pegged to gold but today, it is around $1.3 for every SDR.

Evolution of Policy at the IMF & Lending with Conditionality: the initial idea of creating the Fund was to have a buffer stock of reserves that member countries could draw upon when they had balance of payment issues (did not have sufficient foreign exchange to pay for imports), as a temporary means to fund the deficit. Fundamental conditions of disequilibria[67]

---

66 http://www.imf.org/external/np/exr/facts/sdr.htm

67 A fundamental disequilibrium, for example, would be when a country needed to import petrol and the amount of foreign exchange needed (OPEC required payments to be in US$), was greater than the value of all their exports. Changing the exchange rate could correct it in the following way: If the currency was devalued the cost of the goods they exported in foreign currency would be lower, allowing for enhanced exports (more than enough to cover the loss due to devaluation), and thus the country could earn more foreign exchange to pay

were to be corrected by changing the exchange rate subject to Board approval.

The staff at the IMF made significant contributions towards understanding what constituted fundamental disequilibrium. A number of models were developed to explain the phenomenon. The first important model that emerged was the Absorption Model. This model postulated that the existence of a balance-of-payments deficit implied that the country absorbs (consumes), more resources in consumption and investment than it produces. Based on this idea, they concluded that devaluation of currency would not be sufficient to reverse this trend. Rather, the solution might lie in a decrease in consumption of resources.

This focused analysis on the structure of domestic economies linked it to a country's balance of payments position and required data and policy information of that country. The most important of such frameworks is the Polak Model. An economist at the IMF, Jacques Polak[68] developed a framework which linked balance of payment issues to a country's monetary policy. It was a relatively simple model. The strategy was to decrease absorption by reducing the money supply in a country – this reduction in absorption would help close the balance of payments issue. Typical policies associated with decreasing absorption included raising taxes, increasing interest rates and decreasing overall government expenditure.

This intellectual framework helped develop what is called IMF Conditionality (i.e. the conditions that the IMF imposes on governments and countries that seek funds from it to overcome their balance of payment crises).

---

for petrol imports and correct its balance of payment situation.
68 http://www.imf.org/external/pubs/ft/survey/so/2010/NEW030110A.htm

Conditionality: with the new framework based on the Polak Model in place, the IMF shifted its attention in the late 1950s, away from European economies to the newly emerging economies of the developing world. The Fund defined a set of conditions that member countries had to implement in order to use its funds and this often involved extensive intrusion into the domestic economies of the borrowing nations. These conditions included:

- reduced government spending to reduce domestic consumption
- increasing tax rates and revenues – taking money away from people so they spent less
- raising interest rates which made it more attractive for people to save rather than spend
- liberalizing trade terms and opening up foreign investment – this allowed the country to get foreign exchange which helped in correcting the balance of payments.

Member countries approach the IMF for financial assistance as a lender of last resort[69] when facing a balance-of-payment crisis. IMF loans are disbursed in a number of installments (Reserve + 4 installments) – also known as tranches, over the life of a program – which can typically last up to three years. The first disbursement is known as the Gold or Reserve Tranche, and then the country can avail of the 1st Tranche, which is a quarter of the country's quota denominated in a reserve currency or in SDRs. These two installments are typically available to members with no conditions attached to them. The Second, Third and Fourth tranches, are conditional, with progressively more rigorous requirements for borrowing. When a member seeks these

____

69 When they have no other option or choice, they go to the IMF as the last option

tranches, it must comply with many specific policies put forth by the IMF that are based on the Polak Model discussed previously. The drawing on conditional credit tranches is known as standby arrangements and typically cover a 12-18 month period, and repayments are done within three to five years of each drawing.

This conditionality attached to IMF assistance, has been and is, very controversial, and critics argue that they are driven solely by ideology and a commitment to liberal economic theory or the Washington Consensus. Criticism has also been levelled at the IMF that it uses the same formula for all situations regardless of circumstances that vary from country to country. Most countries shudder at the prospect of these conditions, as they have severe consequences on the domestic economy and the people.

Reducing government spending means cutting essential social support and other programs that help alleviate suffering. Increasing taxes is never popular and more so during times of stress and economic downturns. Also, it is very important to note here that when developed countries such as the US face current account deficits or economic downturns, such as the recent global financial crisis, they do exactly the opposite of what they prescribe through these conditions to developing nations. The US response to the latest crisis: interest rates at 0%, massive government spending increases and rhetoric against liberal policies such as outsourcing.

Over the years, the IMF has periodically created new facilities that member countries have been able to avail of to help with balance of payment crises[70]. These include

---

70 http://www.imf.org/external/pubs/ft/history/2001/ch14.pdf

facilities such as the Compensatory Financing Facility (CFF), to deal with fluctuations in cereal import costs; Buffer Stock Facility (BSF), to help countries finance contributions to international buffer stocks; and others. The most important among these are the Extended Fund Facility (EFF), used to help countries address problems related to structural issues that may take longer to correct (loan repayment terms extended up to seven years), which required countries to improve the way markets and institutions function such as tax and financial sector reforms, privatization of public enterprises and steps to make labor markets more flexible. The Structural Adjustment Facility (SAF) and the Enhanced Structural Adjustment Facility (ESAF), were created along the lines of the EFF but gave them concessional rates for low-income members and for longer periods of up to 10 years. Countries that borrow under these programs commit to a set of long-term conditions outlined in a policy framework paper which includes typical conditions as well as privatizations, deregulation, and a level playing field for foreign investors. IMF also launched the HIPC (Highly Indebted Poor Countries) initiative in 1996, to provide debt relief in a coordinated manner to low income countries and the PRGF (Poverty Reduction and Growth Facility) initiative, to provide 0.5% interest loan for up to 10 years for low income countries.

IMPACT OF IMF ON THE WORLD

The US and its allies promoted their view of the world (the Washington Consensus), through international institutions such as the IMF and instruments such as the Structural Adjustment Programs which forced countries to adopt a more liberal economic system that allowed access for US-based capital and businesses to operate in and profit from. The IMF is more interested in protecting the interests of foreign lenders of capital than the people of the countries they purport to help. IMF structural lending programs pushed countries to liberalize and open their markets, sometimes faster than the societies in these countries could adapt to. The conditionality that came with IMF assistance, caused a lot of hardship and recessions due to the emphasis on lowering absorption by cutting government spending and raising taxes in countries that adopted it.

The resulting recessions, coupled with currency devaluation, make domestic businesses and their assets prime targets for acquisition. By forcing FDI and other liberalization policies, the IMF created the ideal environment for MNCs to walk into a country and profit from its crisis. The IMF in its defense, has said that it is only carrying out its mandate and its policies do resolve balance of payment crises. They also argue that in the long-term, these policies do help countries achieve substantial growth.

Today, most of these countries, such as the Asian Tigers – China and India, and other countries in Latin America, can look back at their market liberalization programs with some satisfaction as their economies have grown significantly but they have also paid dearly for this as can be seen through the lens of multiple crises that emanated from such programs.

Impact on Mexico: in the 1970s, Mexican oil production surpassed 190 million barrels and PEMEX, the national petroleum company, announced discoveries in multiple locations that led President Lopez Portillo, to announce that Mexico had proven reserves of 11 billion barrels. (According to the US Energy Information Administration, Mexico has 10.4

billion barrels of proven oil reserves as of January 2010[71]).

The government decided to increase petroleum production and used the value of their reserves as collateral to acquire large international loans to build onshore and offshore facilities for drilling and processing. Petrol was Mexico's primary source of foreign exchange. A couple of factors, including a recession in the US in 1979, and over-production of oil that led the New York Times in June 1981 to announce the 'Oil Glut'[72], caused price for petrol to drop by more than 60-70%. The impact of falling oil prices and increasing interest rates on international debt, forced Mexico to announce that it was on the verge of defaulting on its foreign debt. This debt crisis also affected many other countries in Latin America, Africa and Asia, and gave the IMF the opportunity to determine the fiscal and monetary policies in many countries around the world.

Mexico negotiated an IMF assistance package with conditionality that included cutting public spending, privatizing government enterprises, and deregulation of its industry. Further agreements with the IMF in 1986 and 1989, cemented this policy path. The IMF, along with the Mexican government and labor unions, also sought to stabilize wages and established a set of social pacts (Pactos), to keep wages in check. For most workers in the 1980s, inflation grew faster than their income, due to these pacts, and their real earnings declined by 75%, leading Mexicans to call the 1980s 'the lost decade'[73]. Government investments in education, R&D and

---

71 http://www.eia.doe.gov/emeu/cabs/Mexico/Oil.html

72 http://www.nytimes.com/1981/06/21/business/how-the-oil-glut-is-changing-business.html

73 Carrasco, Enrique, *1980s: The Debt Crisis & The Lost Decade*, The University of Iowa Center for International Finance & Development http://www.nytimes.com/1981/06/21/business/how-the-oil-glut-is-changing-business.html>

infrastructure were reduced. The government also sold off nearly 1000 public enterprises, most often for a fraction of their value. While this did inject cash into the government in the short run, the privatizations hurt Mexicans over the long run. Multinational companies were the biggest beneficiaries of the fire sale by the Mexican government, acquiring assets built by the country over decades – such as the telephone system. Another of the IMFs policies, import liberalization, hurt a number a small Mexican farmers as industrial grown corn from the US was imported under these policies.

In the early 1990s the Mexican economy started to show signs of improvement but it was relying more and more on foreign capital flows, most of which were short-term portfolio investments. This had another effect, which was to artificially inflate the value of the Mexican Peso, which caused Mexican exports to be more expensive and by mid-1994, foreign investors attacked the Peso by pulling out their money, which put enormous strain on Mexico's foreign exchange reserves[74].

By December 1994, Mexican officials were forced to devalue the Peso and in January 1995, asked the IMF again for assistance. The IMF lent $7.75 Billion and the US Treasury loaned another $18 Billion. The Peso devaluation,

---

74 For example, if the exchange rate before the IMF programs was 1 USD = 100 Pesos, and by liberalizing their capital markets Mexico was able to attract a lot of foreign capital, increasing demand for the Peso and thereby increasing its value to 1 USD = 50 pesos, this would be the scenario – foreign fund A would bring in 1 Million USD to Mexico and convert it to 100 Million Pesos and invest in the capital markets. Mexico now has 1 Million USD of foreign exchange as well. As more and more investors flock to Mexico, the value of the Peso appreciates and now stands at 1USD = 50 Pesos. Fund A, which has 100 Million Pesos, would ask the government to exchange it back to Dollars – which would be 2 Million USD – a cool profit for the Fund and a huge burden on the foreign exchange position for Mexico.

combined with IMF mandated rise in taxes and interest rates, sparked the worst depression in Mexico in 60 years. Millions dropped below the poverty line. Nevertheless, Mexico's GDP has taken off since the mid to late 1990s and except for the year 2009, it has consistently grown to over 1 Trillion USD with a GDP per capita of $9100 and an improving Human Development Index. Looking back today, the policies may seem to have worked but they caused a lot of hardship to the people of Mexico.

Asian Financial Crisis: A similar story can be traced in Asia as well and played out as the Asian Financial Crisis of 1997. Thailand was one the world's poorest countries in the 1950s. In a miraculous transformation of the economy, reminiscent of the Asian Tiger economies (Hong Kong, Singapore, Taiwan and South Korea), its economy grew significantly from 1958 levels and had the fastest growing economy in the world at 10.4% between 1986 and 1996[75]. Exports grew at 14.5% during this decade and inflation averaged a low of 5.3%. By 1997, Thai GNP per capita had reached US $2740[76]. Thailand became the fifth Asian Tiger and its economic model was a showcase for the other emerging nations to emulate.

The backbone of this growth was the passage of the Investment Promotion Act of 1972, favoring exports as the primary driver of the economy. Incentives included those for export and the creation of Export Processing Zones (EPZs), where businesses enjoyed exemption from import and export duties, as well as business taxes. A key component of their monetary policy was to tie the Thai Baht to the US

75 Jitsuchon, Somchai, *Sources of Thailand's Economic Growth: A Fifty Years Perspective (1950-2000),* The Thailand Development Research Institute Foundation <http://depot.gdnet.org/cms/conference/papers/3rd_day2_32_jitsuchon.pdf>
76 'Asian Financial Crisis: Crisis, Reform and Recovery', Shalendra Sharma, Manchester University Press, 2003

Dollar, which later was tied to a basket of currencies though the US Dollar continued to weigh heavily in the basket at approximately 25 Baht for every US Dollar. As the economy continued to grow, it began to attract foreign capital and in the 1980s, capital inflows were $4.5 Billion, which tripled to $14 Billion by 1996[77]. Thailand was one of the chief recipients of Japanese FDI and by 1988, Thailand attracted more FDI than the four Asian Tiger economies.

During the 1980s, Thailand had a number of controls on the repatriation of interest, dividends and the principal of portfolio investment on capital flows into Thailand. Further reforms were made to attract more foreign capital inflows into Thailand, including allowing the purchase of Thai mutual funds, among others. Major changes to these policies came in 1990, when the Bank of Thailand accepted implementation of Article 8 of the IMF agreement, which required Thailand to allow unrestricted transfers with respect to international current transactions. In 1991-92, they liberalized financial controls and by the end of 1992, the repatriation of investment funds was fully liberalized.

By early 1994, all foreign-exchange restrictions on current account transactions were eliminated[78]. These measures promoted massive capital inflows and domestic borrowers were eager to borrow because offshore interest rates were lower than at home. A lot of these inflows were used to speculate in local real estate, as well as in stocks and other local assets, by local players. Banks and financial companies also borrowed heavily in US Dollars in the international market and much of this was in short-term loans ranging from one month to a year.

---

77 Ibid 74
78 Ibid 75

The Thai economy was now integrated with the world financial system. The Mexican Peso crisis in 1994, as well as other internal research, indicated that Thailand had a dangerous mix of capital market liberalization coupled with a fixed exchange rate policy. As shown in the Peso crisis, this massive inflow of FDI creates inflation of assets and any quick and massive outflow of foreign capital places a huge strain on the foreign exchange reserves of the country, often leading to devaluation of the currency and a balance of payments crisis. This high rate of capital flows was reflected in Thailand's skyrocketing external debt, which jumped to over US$100 Billion by mid-1997.

This huge debt, coupled with the fact that most of it was short-term, put Thailand at risk of liquidity shortage should creditors decide not to roll over maturing debt. The result of this massive expansion of money in Thailand was a classic real estate bubble with asset pricing rising much above its economic value and a massive private current account deficit. The crisis started when exports began slowing down in 1996 and the real estate bubble burst, bankrupting many real estate companies and saddling banks and financial institutions with bad debt. This combination of widening current account deficit, export slowdown and worsening debt situation, caused widespread expectation that the central bank could no longer support the fixed exchange rate. Foreign investors began moving their money out of Thailand.

The first to collapse was the Bangkok Bank of Commerce, and soon foreign speculators began attacking the Baht. In December 2006, more than 500 companies on the stock exchange reported declining earnings, sparking another round of foreign capital exit from Thailand.

International hedge funds such as Soros's Quantum Fund and other US financial institutions such as JP Morgan and Goldman, took speculative short positions on the Baht, causing the Bank of Thailand to expend much of the country's foreign reserves in shoring up the value of the Baht and by the end of June, Thailand's net foreign-exchange reserves stood at only $2.8 Billion. In July, Thailand announced the Baht was being decoupled from the US Dollar and its value plummeted 18%. In late July, Thai authorities requested the IMF for assistance.

The IMF approved a 3-year $17.2 Billion loan package, along with the regular conditions which included tight monetary and fiscal policies and increasing VAT (value added tax) from 7 to 10%. The impact of these conditions, combined with the bursting of the real estate bubble and the resulting recession, was devastating. Thailand's GDP contracted from $182 Billion in 1996 to $112 Billion in 1998, and it was clear that Thailand was in much deeper recession than had been anticipated when the IMF package was put in place. Unemployment rose, real wages declined and the Baht continued its downward path. Real recovery did not begin until 2001-2002.

More importantly, the Thai crisis triggered an Asia-wide crisis, a phenomenon economists refer to as 'the contagion effect'. Soon, Indonesia's Rupiah was under attack by speculators betting that Indonesia too would have problems. The Indonesian government went to great lengths to assure investors that Indonesia was not Thailand and indeed they were not. They had a positive current account balance, low levels of external debt and large foreign exchange reserves of $20 Billion. Nevertheless, relentless speculative attacks coupled with high domestic demand for foreign exchange, forced the government to abandon their exchange rate policies and devalue the Rupiah.

On 31 October 1997, the Indonesian government negotiated a financial bailout package totaling some US $43 Billion, with the IMF and other donors – with extensive conditions attached to them. With IMF technical assistance, the government shutdown 12 banks, which triggered a massive panic and quickly became a full blown financial crisis. The resulting contraction of economic activity of 15%, was the most severe economic collapse recorded since the great depression of 1929. Rising unemployment and huge inflation led to widespread rioting in several major cities and towns throughout the country.

A similar story repeated itself in Malaysia and speculators attacked the Ringgit, forcing it to lose value and affect the stock market as well as the real economy. Former Malaysian Prime Minister, Mahathir Mohamed, accused George Soros, of ruining Malaysia's economy with massive currency speculation. While other countries in Asia were affected by this contagion, let's look at one last country: South Korea.

When the crisis hit Thailand, Indonesia and others, it was widely believed that South Korea would not be affected. South Korea had the second largest economy in Asia, with good domestic savings, a positive fiscal position (government spent less than it earned in taxes and other income), and a small current account deficit. The Korean economy though, was controlled by large conglomerates known as Chaebols, which had borrowed heavily to invest in industries and other enterprises. The bankruptcy of the Hanbo Group, Korea's 14th largest Chaebol, exposed some of the problems in the economy.

In the following government investigations, eight more of Korea's top 30 Chaebols crashed, including Kia Motors. At the end of 1996, Korea's foreign debt stood at $180 Billion, of which $130 was payable within a year[79]. The softness in the export markets that hit Thailand affected Korea too. The Asian Flu soon spread to Korea and investors began withdrawing money. The growing flight of capital sent the Korean Won down to record lows. The Bank of Korea intervened heavily but this only resulted in the depletion of foreign exchange reserves.

In mid-November 1997, the IMF's Managing Director, Michel Camdessus, travelled to South Korea and on 3 December 1997, details of an IMF brokered package of $57 Billion was announced. As usual this assistance came with strings and conditions that included higher taxes, higher interest rates and reduced government spending, as well as financial and market restructuring. The IMF also insisted on a complete restructuring of the businesses away from the Chaebol model. The ensuing financial crisis paralyzed banks and sent consumers into a panic. The conditions imposed by the IMF led to a severe economic contraction and the unemployment rate jumped from 2.5% to 8.5%. An estimated 10,000 workers were losing jobs each day[80] and at least one small business owner committing suicide every day. The Koreans angrily criticized the IMF for interfering in their economy and banners read, 'IMF = I Am Fired'. South Korea dropped from being the world's 11th largest economy to 17th position, in a matter of weeks.

---

79 'Managing the Asian Meltdown: The IMF and South Korea', Gregory P. Corning, Santa Clara University, Institute for the study of Diplomacy, 2000
80 San-hun Choe, 'Hyundai sets 20 percent work force cut:', *The Washington Post*, 10 April 1998

Many critics, including Nobel Prize winner Joseph Stieglitz, and Harvard professor Jeffrey Sachs, have argued that the IMF blindly implemented incorrect policies in response to the Asian crisis, prolonging the recession and causing untold hardships. The crisis in South Korea was one of short-term capital crunch and not excessive government spending or excess absorption in the domestic economy. The IMF prescriptions were totally out of line with the nature of the crisis and led South Korea into its worst post-war economic crisis. Nevertheless, by the start of 1999, Korea enjoyed its first quarter of growth since the crisis and continued to grow rapidly, re-establishing South Korea as a dominant economy.

Most of Asia was able to navigate the financial crisis of 2007-9 fairly well, emerging quickly, which the IMF has claimed was due to the restructuring that happened during the Asian Financial Crisis. At the Asia 21 Conference in Korea (2010), the Managing Director of the IMF, Dominique Strauss-Kahn, said in reference to the role the IMF has played in helping make the Asian economy resilient, "The macroeconomic, financial and corporate sector reforms put in place over the last decade have played an important role in the region's resilience. So, despite being hit hard initially, Asia was able to bounce back quickly from the global financial crisis"[81]. A question still remains though: was a Washington Consensus driven IMF policy really needed for South Korea or were there other motives behind those policies?

India & the IMF: the early years of independence were particularly difficult times for India economically. India was not self-sufficient in food and had to depend on foreign aid

------

81 http://www.business-standard.com/india/news/holdbubbly-go-afterbubble-imf-cautions-asia/401253/

to import food. The Government of India ran large fiscal deficits and the wars with China in 1962 and with Pakistan in 1965, took away precious capital from investments and into defense-related spending. Draughts in 1965/66 and 1971/72, currency devaluations, and the first world oil crisis in 1973, all put enormous strain on the Indian economy.

In 1965, India faced severe draughts. Reports of food shortages loomed across India. The Indian government requested a two-year food aid agreement with the US. India's then Prime Minister, Indira Gandhi, travelled to the US to negotiate with US President, Lyndon Johnson. The outcome was a bargain that if India adopted economic reforms, devalued its currency, and supported or remained neutral to the US operations in Vietnam, than the US would, through the World Bank and IMF, provide the necessary resources to ensure food security.[82]

By mid-1965, the Indian economy was approaching a serious balance of payments crisis and exchange reserves fell to critical levels. India had no choice but to deal with the IMF and borrowed $200 Million. IMF conditionality came along with the loan and India agreed to devalue its currency, cut fiscal/government expenditure and tighten credit, as well as consider import liberalization. Details of this agreement became public in 1966, and there was a huge outcry from the Indian press, the Left political parties and others, against the infringement of Indian sovereignty by the IMF. The government had to abandon critical components of the package due to intense domestic opposition and by 1967, most of India's aid donors withdrew their pledges

82 'The Evolution of Home Grown Conditionality in India: IMF Relations', P.K. Chaudhry, Vijay Kelkar & Vikash Yadav, *The Journal of Development Studies*, Vol 40, No. 6, August 2004

of support. The first attempt at reform was abandoned. A confluence of events in 1979, drove India towards another fiscal crisis. These included:

1. the Iranian revolution and the resulting second oil crisis which pushed petrol prices higher
2. a draught that severely affected agricultural production
3. political instability and Indira Gandhi elected Prime Minister again in 1980.

Drawing upon the previous experience of domestic resistance to getting assistance from the IMF, the new government undertook a strategy called 'Homegrown Conditionality'. Instead of letting the IMF dictate conditionality for assistance, the Indian government incorporated some aspects of the conditionality clauses into the Sixth 5-Year Plan and privately ascertained if the IMF would lend based on these plans. The IMF in turn, learning from the past and recognizing that this would be the only way to gain a foothold in India, agreed to the terms.

The Sixth 5-Year Plan, with built-in assumptions of the IMF loan, was presented to the Indian Parliament, making the process more transparent than in other countries. In November 1981, India received assistance from the IMF: the largest package to be given to a developing country, at around $6 Billion, over a three-year period. India recovered from the crisis and when production of petrol from Bombay High commenced in 1984, India's foreign exchange crisis came to a temporary halt. India demonstrated to the world that Homegrown Conditionality could be a sustainable practice for economic reforms in a democratic society. The growing interaction between the IMF and the Government of India officials and intellectuals would set the stage for another set of homegrown reforms in 1991. From the 1980s, a number of Indian economists held various positions at the IMF and many enhanced their skills at the institution including Shankar Acharya, Suman Bery and Montek Singh Ahluwalia, who spent the first 11 years of his career at the IMF before returning to India in 1991, to serve as Finance Secretary.

The 1991 Crisis: India faced a perfect storm of difficulties in 1991. Iraq invaded Kuwait, resulting in the First Gulf War, which drove up the price of petrol. The Soviet Union, which was one of India's largest trading partners, broke up, leading to a steep drop in economic activity. The US and Canada were reeling under a recession, and a major political crisis erupted in India when Rajiv Gandhi was assassinated by a LTTE suicide mission in May 1991.

The Gulf crisis had multiple impacts on India. The rising cost of petrol stroked domestic inflation and depleted foreign exchange reserves. There was a dramatic fall in foreign currency remittances from Indian workers in the Gulf, most of whom had to be airlifted by the government from the conflict zone, further hurting foreign exchange reserves. Towards the end of 1990, Prime Minister VP Singh, was forced to resign when the BJP withdrew support and a new government led by Chandrashekhar was sworn in. Chandrashekar's Samajwadi Janata Party lasted all of six months[83] in power and fresh elections were called when the Congress party withdrew its support, leading to political instability. This instability affected investments into the country and the slowdown in trade with the Soviet Union and the US, placed further strain on India's foreign exchange reserves.

---

83 http://pmindia.nic.in/former.htm

The increasing burden of current account deficits, coupled with high government fiscal deficits at 9.4% of GDP, which was financed by external borrowing, quickly led to the depletion of India's foreign exchange reserves and the ballooning of external debt. In the period between July-September 1990, the government sought assistance from the IMF from the reserve tranche for $660 Million.

Again in January 1991, the Government made another drawing of $1.025 Billion under the CCF facility and $789 Million under a first credit tranche arrangement[84] (recall that these are given without any conditionality attached). Nevertheless, by January 1991, India had only $896 Million of foreign exchange reserves[85] and that declined by over 50% by June 1991 – barely enough to cover 2-3 weeks of imports.

By June, the balance of payments crisis became a crisis of confidence in India's ability to repay external debt, which closed off access to all sources of credit. A default on payments for the first time in India's history, became a real possibility.

In May, the interim government of Chandrashekar, allowed the State Bank of India to sell 20 tonnes of gold with a six-month repurchase option and in July the newly formed government under PV Narasimha Rao, authorized the Reserve Bank of India to ship 47 tonnes of gold to the Bank of England, to raise about $600 Million in all[86]. It was evident that the economy needed substantial reforms to overcome India's persistent balance of payments problems.

The new Prime Minister, Narasimha Rao, put together

84 http://indiabudget.nic.in/es1991-92_A/2%20The%20Payments%20Crisis.pdf
85 http://indiabudget.nic.in/es1991-92_A/2%20The%20Payments%20Crisis.pdf
86 http://indiabudget.nic.in/es1991-92_A/2%20The%20Payments%20Crisis.pdf

a team of technocrats to deal with the problem, including appointing Manmohan Singh as Finance Minister, Montek Singh Ahluwalia as Secretary, Department of Economic Affairs and Raja Chelliah, as Minister of State. Another advocate of reforms, C. Rangarajan, was appointed RBI Governor in 1992 and in 1993, Shankar Acharya was called in from the World Bank as Chief Economic Advisor. This elite team of technocrats, with strong relationships at the IMF/WB, put together a series of homegrown conditionality reforms in the subsequent budgets.

In August 1991, the government approached the IMF again and a standby arrangement for $2.3 Billion over 20 months was secured, based on the homegrown conditionality built into the budget by the government. India undertook wideranging reforms but at a slower pace than typical IMF conditionality demanded. These reforms included dismantling the 'license *raj*' and liberalization of many aspects of the economy including capital controls and FDI. The Rupee was devalued and it fell from Rs17.5 per USD in 1991 to Rs 45 per USD in 1992[87].

The economy and FDI inflows began to grow and exports as well as new industries such as IT, began to expand rapidly. Reserves soon climbed and by the end of 1993, economic growth recovered enough so that India did not have to extend the IMF standby agreement beyond 1993. Attempts to reign in fiscal deficits culminated in the Fiscal Responsibility and Budget Management Act of 2003[88]. The reform process continued in subsequent years and under different governments, which helped India grow rapidly to reach a GDP of more than 1 Trillion USD and have foreign

---

87 http://en.wikipedia.org/wiki/1991_India_economic_crisis#cite_note-3
88 http://www.rediff.com/money/2006/nov/30guest.htm

exchange reserves of over $250 Billion by 2009. India was not affected severely by the Asian Financial Crisis in 1997 and has since emerged as the fourth largest economy in PPP terms and the 11th largest in nominal USD terms. Ownership of the reform process allowed India to set its own pace of reforms – a strategy that is now being promoted within the IMF by India and other countries.

In a complete reversal of fortune, India bought 200 tonnes of gold from the IMF for $6.7 Billion in 2009[89], in a move which surprised many analysts. Bimal Jalan, a former Governor of the Reserve Bank of India, said the move was aimed at increasing liquidity at the IMF so that it could increase low cost lending to other developing countries. It was also a show of strength by India, who is demanding reforms at the IMF and a greater say in its operations. In complete contrast, Greece, a member of the EU ,is facing a severe balance of payments crisis largely due to high fiscal deficit and has had to take the help of the IMF to restructure its economy. The assistance has come with the standard conditions that are attached to IMF loans (i.e. a government austerity package that has prompted massive protest and public unrest throughout May, 2010[90]). Other EU members, including Spain, Portugal and Ireland, face similar fiscal deficit crises and the very stability of the Euro is under threat.

REFORMS AT THE IMF

There are calls for two distinctive sets of reforms at the IMF. One is to modify the conditionality requirements to suit local conditions (i.e. to allow governments to set their own homegrown conditionality), and the second is to change the power structure of the governing body of the IMF.

---

89 New York Times, November 3, 2009
90 http://www.brettonwoodsproject.org/art.shtml?x=566356

Over the last few years, small but significant changes have occurred in the power structure of the financial world, including the replacement of the G8 (Group of the 8 most industrialized nations), with the G20 (far more representative of countries around the world), as a forum for co-operation and consultation on matters pertaining to the international financial system, including the IMF. An ad-hoc change in quotas was made in 2006, to correct under-represented economies such as China, Turkey, Korea and Mexico[91] (nevertheless, China is still under-represented at the IMF, given that it is the second largest economy in the world. It has voting rights similar to small European economies such as Belgium and the Netherlands).

The G20 summits have called for reforms to the IMF as well and there are proposals to increase the quotas of developing countries by 5.4%, while reducing the quotas of the industrialized nations. In 2009, at the Fund's annual meeting, the BRIC countries said they were willing to contribute to a quadrupling of IMF resources to $1 Trillion by purchasing bonds – a sign of strength as well as backing up their demands for increased quotas and a greater say at the IMF.

India has called for a shift of at least 7% in quota shares in favor of developing economies and D. Subbarao, the Governor of the RBI, has said that only such a substantial shift would better reflect current global economic realities and enhance the legitimacy of the IMF[92]. The IMF has committed to completing governance and quota reform before January 2011. The IMF must also implement more transparent processes, including appointments of personnel

---

91 http://www.imf.org/external/np/exr/ib/2007/041307.htm
92 http://ibnlive.in.com/news/india-demands-greater-say-at-imf-world-bank/
113946-2.html

and details of discussions held at the Executive Board. The practice of always appointing a European Managing Director must also be discontinued in favour of a more democratic process. A combination of readjustment of quotas and consequently voting rights, more transparency in operations and appointments, along with a strategy based on homegrown conditionality, may be just the right mix of changes needed to make the IMF a more just international organization, with the legitimacy and effectiveness needed in today's complex financial world.

THE WORLD BANK

The World Bank Group is a sister organization of the IMF and was created along with it at the Bretton Woods Conference. Countries have to be members of the IMF before they can be associated with the World Bank Group. The World Bank Group consists of 5 primary organizations: IBRD (International Bank for Reconstruction and Development); IDA (International Development Association); IFC (International Finance Corporation); MIGA (Multilateral Investment Guarantee Agency); and ICSID (International Center for Settlement of Investment Disputes). The IBRD and the IDA together are typically referred to as the World Bank.

IBRD: the International Bank For Reconstruction And Development was the first entity to be created in 1945. Its main purpose was to aid the reconstruction of war-torn Europe and Japan. While the IMF was envisioned as a provider of short-term loans to adjust balance of payment imbalances, the World Bank was created to provide longer term loans to aid in reconstruction of economies. IBRD provides loans at favourable rates and raises most of its funds on the world's financial markets through bonds.

During its first years of operation, the World Bank lent mainly to industrialized countries in Europe. France was the World Bank's initial customer, with a loan of $250 Million.

The World Bank's lending policy to Europe was radically changed with the introduction of the Marshall Plan in 1948. The World Bank changed its focus to development activities to help fight poverty and under-development in the developing world. The World Bank supported and helped finance many large infrastructure projects, as well as partnered with the IMF to impose conditionality on countries that wanted its help.

There is also a lot of criticism of the role the World Bank played during the Cold War, for its support to many dictators and oppressive regimes, only because they were allies of the US. Criticism has also been levied that most of the large projects it supported, were environment disasters, with little regard for local populations – such as the Narmada Valley Project. The purposes of the Bank as stated in its Article 1[93] are:

1. To assist in the reconstruction and development of members by facilitating the investment of capital for the development of productive facilities and resources in less developed countries.
2. To promote foreign investment by means of guarantees or participation in loans and to promote the growth of international trade thereby assisting in raising standard of living.

IDA: the second component of the World Bank is the International Development Agency – which was established

---

93 http://web.worldbank.org/WBSITE/EXTERNAL/EXTABOUTUS/0,,contentMD
K:20049563~pagePK:43912~menuPK:58863~piPK:36602,00.html#I1

in 1960, to provide long-term loans, coupled with aid, to the poorest countries that could not afford to pay the interest rate being charged by IBRD. IDA is the principle agency of the World Bank that provides zero % loans with long maturities, targeted at countries with low GDP per capita (less than $875).

Funding for IDA's activities comes from donations by member countries as well as the profits made by the IBRD and repayments of IDA loans. IDA loans address issues related to human development, including primary education, basic health, water etc, and IDA is a key institution within the World Bank Group to help countries striving to meet the Millennium Development goals. IDA is one of the largest sources of assistance for the world's poorest countries, a majority of whom are in Asia and Africa.

IFC: while IBRD and IDA lend to governments, the IFC was created in 1956, to promote economic development through the private sector. IFC invests in sustainable private enterprises in developing countries, without any government guarantees. It is the largest multilateral source of loan and equity financing for private sector projects in developing countries and seeks to reach businesses in regions and countries that have limited access to capital. IFC charges market rates for its loans and to be eligible, projects must be profitable. IFC's share capital is provided by member countries and it also raises capital in the markets.

MIGA: the Multilateral Investment Guarantee Agency encourages foreign investment in developing countries by providing guarantees to foreign investors against losses caused by political risk or breach of contract. It was established in 1988. MIGA also helps countries market their investment opportunities to international players. In countries such as Chad, where the political situation is very unstable and which deters any investment coming into the country, MIGA provides the risk insurance companies need, to make investment decisions that benefit not only the company but also the local population.

Many critics have argued though, that the great majority of benefits are appropriated by the international companies and very little is left behind. Many investment projects in the least developed countries typically are resource extraction projects such as mining for valuable metals and minerals or petroleum exploration and extraction. While the governments of these countries make some money through royalty and taxes, the local population is often displaced and ends up with small and labour wage jobs, while the multinational companies benefit the most. Proponents have argued that without the involvement of MIGA, IFC and other branches of the World Bank, the project would never have started and the benefits to the government and people would not exist.

ICSID: the International Centre for Settlement of Investment Disputes, helps encourage foreign investment by providing facilities for reconciliation and arbitration of investment disputes between States and foreign investors. It was established in 1966.

The structure and governance of the World Bank is very similar to the IMF. The World Bank has a Board of Governors (similar to the IMF), an Executive Board with five appointed members and 19 elected members (similar to the IMF), and a President (equivalent to the Managing Director at the IMF), who traditionally has always been an American, appointed by the US President, and ratified by the Executive Board. Voting rights at the World Bank are also based on subscription values and the US again, is the only country with veto power, able to single-handedly block major changes.

Impact of the WB: the World Bank has been involved in many projects around the world since its inception. In the initial years, up till the mid-to-late 1960s, the World Bank primarily did project lending to governments in developing countries to build dams, roads, ports and other infrastructure projects. Very little focus was given to social service projects or agriculture. Many have argued that this focus on development, displaced many local populations, damaged the environment and led to many social problems in the countries where the projects were implemented. Proponents have argued on the basis of good for the majority. When Robert McNamara became President of the World Bank, he led the shift from project-based to program-based lending and targeted poverty reduction as a main goal for the World Bank. The IDA took on the primary role of channeling funds for poverty reduction and health, food and education projects.

In the 1980s, the Bank's approach almost merged with that of the IMF and they would lend together, based on conditionalities attached to their assistance. The IMF also began to have a number of longer term development loans and the roles of the IMF and the WB began to blur.

The James Wolfensohn era of 1995-2005, introduced the CDF or Comprehensive Development Framework, that expanded the role of the Bank to deal with corruption, institution building and incorporated extensive consultations with NGOs. Since 2000, when the UN Millennium General

Assembly adopted the Millennium Development Goals targeted at reducing poverty in all its forms, they provided a focus for the efforts of the World Bank Group and other multilateral organizations. The Millennium Goals are to halve the number of people living on less than one Dollar a day, in extreme poverty; achieve universal primary education; promote gender equality; reduce child mortality by two-thirds; reduce maternal mortality by two-thirds; reverse the spread of HIV/AIDS, Malaria and other major diseases; halve the number of people without access to potable water; and improve the lives of slum dwellers; and develop a global partnership for development. The World Bank collects a number of statistics on these Goals for every country and the information is available on their website: www.worldbank.org

India & the WB: India has been one of the World Bank's biggest recipients of funds and assistance. The World Bank's plan is spelt out in its country strategy, which is aligned with the Indian governments Eleventh Five-Year Plan. The Plan for 2009-12, calls for World Bank funding to the tune of $14 Billion and there are currently 75 active projects in many different areas and sectors, with total commitments to the tune of $21.4 Billion[94].

Some of the projects include a dedicated freight corridor ($1.8 Billion in loans from IBRD); the Ganga River Basin Authority ($1 Billion from IDA); Rural Roads projects ($1.5 billion from the ID); and the National Highways project, with $1 Billion in loans from the IBRD. The IFC has also invested heavily in India and its portfolio of $2.3 Billion

---

94 http://www.worldbank.org.in/WBSITE/EXTERNAL/COUNTRIES/SOUTHASIAEXT/ INDIAEXTN/0,,contentMDK:22019695~pagePK:141137~piPK:141127~theSite PK:295584,00.html

in investments makes India its third largest country of operations[95]. IFC has given loans to more than 199 different projects run by various companies, including the TATAs, Moser Baer and others[96].

Of the many projects that have been financed or been assisted by the World Bank some of the more prominent ones include the development of the Singrauli region in central India for power generation and transmission; the Bihar Plateau Development Project; The Damodar Valley Project; and the Narmada Valley Project. There have been concerns about environmental damage and displacement of local populations as well as the direct benefits aggregated to multinational companies which supply most of the technology, machinery and direction to a number of World Bank funded projects around the world; other issues of debate include corruption and misuse of these funds and the growing debt trap. In countries like India, where corruption in political life is rampant, a good percentage of the loan ends up lost in corruption. This adversely impacts the viability of these projects and the people of the country are stuck with repaying these loans. One must question the governance of these projects and ensure there is more transparency in the disbursement and use of these loans.

FINAL THOUGHTS

The growing confidence of the BRIC countries, coupled with financial troubles in the developed nations, is forcing a number of reforms to be discussed at the IMF and World Bank. India's economy has recovered quickly from the recession of 2007-2009 and is on track to grow by more than 9% in 2010. This confidence has allowed India to

---

95 http://www.ifc.org/ifcext/southasia.nsf/Content/India_overview
96 http://www.ifc.org/ifcext/southasia.nsf/Content/ProjectInformationIndia

purchase huge quantities of gold from the IMF.

India has also shown that homegrown conditionality is a more appropriate way to introduce reforms in developing countries – allowing each country to create its own path and to ensure the democratic process and sovereignty of the country are not violated. As a growing regional economic power, India must help its neighbours partake in its success and aid their growth by giving them access to India's vast market, as well as technologies developed in India, that are more suitable for use in developing economies.

The TATA Nano, is a great example of Indian technology that is more suitable to developing countries and their need for affordable transportation rather than what has been developed in Western countries. Indian companies must take advantage of their relationships with the IFC to invest in neighbouring countries such as Nepal, Sri Lanka and even Pakistan. India and the other BRIC countries, must challenge the Dollar's role as the reserve currency of the world and work towards one that is based on a basket of currencies. Reforms at the IMF and WB to restructure the decision-making process and meaningfully change the quotas, must be pursued. India can and should promote the idea of an Indian/New Delhi Consensus to counter the Washington Consensus – one that includes homegrown conditionality; collective action and support (both technical and resources) from the BRIC and other developing countries; reform and restructuring of the IMF and the WB to make them more representative and democratic – with a focus on both economic and social development.

WTO & India's Place
in the World of Global Trade

4

The idea that trade between countries should be free from governmental intervention, is actually quite new compared to the history of international trade itself. Mercantilist (economic nationalist) policies were employed to create positive balance of trade positions and contribute to State Power, while State Power was often used to protect countries' trading activities. Trade contributed to State Power through the wealth it generated and State's Power was used to protect and grow trade. It was a symbiotic relationship.

Many European nations built powerful navies to protect their trading ships and established trading posts in countries around the world. Modern trade liberalization (i.e. freeing trade from state imposed restrictions), can be traced back to bilateral treaties that were signed in the 19th century between the newly industrializing nations in Europe. One of the first was the Cobden-Chevalier[97] Treaty of 1860, between Britain and France, to reduce tariffs on goods traded between them. During the second half of the 19th century,

---

97 Richard Peet, *Unholy Trinity, The IMF, World Bank and WTO*, Zed Books, London, 2009

international trade expanded rapidly as the colonial powers acquired colonies around the world and exchanged goods with them and amongst themselves. After the end of the First World War, most countries devastated by the physical and economic costs of the war, began to revert to mercantilist policies and then in 1929, the stock market in New York crashed and a period of severe economic contraction, or the Great Depression, began around the world.

Two of the major causes that prolonged the duration and severity of the Great Depression have been attributed to competitive currency devaluations and raising import tariffs which were aimed at reducing imports and boosting exports. These protectionist policies were implemented by countries hoping to gain an unfair advantage in global trade, but the response was that everyone else enacted similar policies and no one gained in the process and prolonging the depression. The effect of acts such as the Smoot-Hawley Tariff Act, was devastating to global trade. When the US began designing a new architecture for the financial and trade world, they envisioned a trio of international organizations that would prevent a reoccurrence of the Great Depression – the IMF, which would stabilize currency exchange rates; the World Bank, which would help post-war reconstruction in Europe and speed them on their journey to rejoin global trade; and the ITO (International Trade Organization), which would ensure free trade and ensure that mercantilist policies did not find their way back to haunt international trade.

The IMF and World Bank were conceptualized at the Bretton Woods cCnference in 1944, and at the proposal of the US, the United Nations Economic and Social Committee adopted a resolution in 1946, calling for a conference to draft a charter for the International Trade Organization.

ITO

The US published a draft of the ITO charter. The first preparatory committee meeting to discuss the charter was set for October 1946, in London. The main conference to discuss the ITO charter was held in Geneva in 1947, and was followed by the final meeting in Havana, Cuba in 1948. The negotiations on the ITO charter were successfully completed in Havana and provided for the establishment of the ITO as well as set out the basic rules for international trade. An Interim Commission for the ITO, ICITO, was set up in Geneva, Switzerland.

However, the US Congress failed to approve the ITO charter and the US never joined the organization. Without the membership of the US, the largest economy of the time, the ITO was doomed to fail and it never took off. The US was particularly unhappy about the amendments made to the charter it had originally proposed at the UN conferences and was not willing to grant authority of such an important issue (trade), to the UN, where it did not enjoy special voting privileges, unlike at the IMF and WB.

GATT

As the US began to understand the nature and causes of the Great Depression, it began to undertake bilateral trade treaties to start opening up trade with selected countries. The US Congress enacted the Reciprocal Trade Agreements Act in 1934, and gave the US President the authority to enter into reciprocal agreements to lower tariffs. The US entered into bilateral trade pacts with the UK, Canada and Argentina, among others, and by 1945, had entered into 32 bilateral agreements reducing tariffs[98]. Later versions of these agreements formed the basis of most of the clauses in GATT.

---

98   'Restructuring the GATT System', John H Jackson, Royal Institute of International Affairs, 1990

The conference in Geneva in 1947, to discuss the ITO charter, was in fact, the venue of three separate discussions. In addition to discussing the ITO charter, a second meeting dealt with the negotiation of multilateral agreements to reduce tariffs. A third meeting concentrated on drafting the general clauses of obligations for nations to refrain from a variety of trade-impeding measures. The original idea was for these agreements and obligations to be monitored under the ITO charter. The US Congress rejected the ITO charter and did not ratify the US joining it – but could not prevent the US President from accepting (based on the 1934 act), the Multilateral Agreements and the General Clauses of Obligations for trade, which together formed the basis for GATT.

So GATT, without a charter, was born out of political compulsions in the US, where the President was authorized to negotiate bilateral agreements but did not have the authority to enter into agreement for an organization. GATT came into effect in 1947, and as it is basically a set of contracts, all members of GATT are referred to as Contracting Parties (CPs). Since the ITO never materialized, the GATT soon became the central institution for international trade and the ICITO (Commission for ITO), became GATT's *de facto* secretariat. From being a set of agreements, GATT soon became an established code for international commerce. But as it was primarily a trade treaty, there was no provision in it for an organized structure or for it to become an international organization – a deficiency that would later be overcome by the WTO.

GATT regulated trade in (manufactured) goods, using agreed-upon principles of liberalization, equal market access, reciprocity, non-discrimination and transparency.

The basic idea behind GATT was to eliminate or reduce protectionism or mercantilism and promote international trade between countries, which would lead to increasing the level of economic growth everywhere (based on the liberal philosophy).

GUIDING PRINCIPLES OF GATT

One of the guiding principles of the GATT agreement is non-discrimination, set out in Article I as the Most Favored Nations (MFN) clause and in Article III, as the National Treatment clause. Under the MFN clause, countries cannot normally discriminate between their trading partners (i.e. if a country grants a special favour to one of its partners, such as a lower customs duty rate, then it must offer it to all GATT CPs). Some exceptions are allowed and were negotiated into the agreements at various rounds, such as giving developing countries special access to markets in the US and EU.

The MFN clause means that every time a country lowers a trade barrier or opens up a market, it has to do so for all its trading partners – whether rich or poor, weak or strong.[99] The principle of National Treatment is set out in Article 3, which states that imported and locally produced goods should be treated equally once the foreign goods have entered the market. That is, once a foreign-made good has entered a domestic market, local laws should not discriminate against it, such as not giving it distribution access or taxing it additionally without taxing similar locally-made products. GATT articles also provided contracting parties protection from imports if they were subjected

---

99 http://www.wto.org/english/thewto_e/whatis_e/tif_e/utw_chap1_e.pdf

to dumping[100]. Article VI[101] allows contracting parties to apply duties and other measures to goods originating in member countries, which are dumped and/or enjoy export subsidies[102] to specific conditions. Article X1X[103], also known as the Safeguards clause, allows CPs to take remedial measures including suspension of imports, if the volume of imports can be shown to be injurious or detrimental to domestic industries.

Another guiding principle has been the predictability of rules and trade barriers which encourages investment and growth of trade and prosperity. The principle of transparency declared that protectionist measures employed by governments should be clearly stated and be visible – such as an import tariff, rather than take the shape of a non-tariff barrier – such as systematic refusal by customs authorities to let the goods enter the country. GATT also promoted trade negotiations as a means of encouraging countries to lower trade barriers and reciprocate tariff and other concessions. Since GATT's creation in 1947-48, there have been eight rounds of trade negotiations between contracting parties and at the eighth round in Uruguay the GATT system paved the way for the WTO (World Trade Organization).

Dispute Resolution: the GATT system of agreements also allowed for members to bring forth disputes with other

---

100 'Dumping' refers to the practice when a manufacturer exports a product to another country at a price lower than the price it charges in its domestic market or less than the cost of its manufacture. Also referred to as 'predatory pricing', it is employed to either gain market share in the foreign country or unfairly kill competition.

101 http://www.wto.org/english/docs_e/legal_e/gatt47_02_e.htm

102 An export subsidy is given by a domestic trade policy (government), to promote exports such as lower or no taxes. This makes the product less expensive and better able to compete in international markets.

103 See 63

members to be resolved as per Article XXIII[104]. The article has three main features – any contracting party must first try to resolve any dispute with the other party/parties bilaterally. If the bilateral negotiations do not result in a satisfactory outcome the matter may be brought before the GATT. GATT shall investigate the matter and if they deem the circumstances serious enough to justify action, may authorize a contracting party or parties to take effective remedial measures. The contracting party that is at the receiving end of these remedial measures, may choose to leave the agreement by giving a written notice no later than 60 days after such action is taken.

During the initial years, disputes were generally taken up by the biannual plenary meeting of the contracting parties. Later, they were brought up before Intercessional Committees or dispute panels, set up by the contracting parties. The dispute panels typically consisted of experts not representing any government and submitted their reports to the contracting parties for final approval.

All approvals at GATT were based on consensus and had to be agreed to by all parties. This made the dispute settlement process at GATT a weak one as losing parties often blocked adoption of the panel report. Moreover, the panel rulings were not binding and in general, the dispute resolution mechanism under GATT was regarded to be weak and not very effective. The use of GATT dispute settlement procedures remained sporadic and declined in the 1960s. But the US began to bring a number of cases to GATT in the 1970s.

---

104 See 63

US Congress Takes Action

The US was the most dominant economy and trading partner in the world in the 1950s and 1960s, running positive current account balances every year. The US led the international system and the Marshall Plan helped Europe and Japan to rebuild their economies. Until the 1960s, the US helped the recovery and development in Japan by keeping the US market open to Japanese goods even though the Japanese market was essentially closed to American goods.

The 1970s was a period of turmoil for the US: the oil crisis in 1973 and the resulting recession caused stagflation (high unemployment and high inflation). The US suffered heavy losses, both human and financial, in the Vietnam War, and the rise of Japan and other Asian export-driven economies, led to a decline of US dominance in world trade. While the US remained the largest economy and the biggest trader in the world, it began to experience current account deficits[105].

This change in fortunes promoted the rise of protectionist voices in the US, especially in vulnerable industries such as textiles, steel, footwear etc. Industries organized special interest groups to further their cause. These groups put pressure on the US Congress and the President for relief from foreign competition. The number of complaints and disputes that the US raised at GATT grew in the 1970s. Frustrated by the lack of an effective dispute settlement process at GATT, the US Congress took matters into its own hands to protect its domestic and sovereign interests.

---

105 Imports exceeded exports and the country was essentially losing money in international trade

Important aspects of the US trade policy were embodied in the US Trade Act of 1974. Under this act, the Office of the US Trade Representative, was created as a cabinet level position with the task of monitoring and co-ordinating US trade policy. This office also conducted investigations into the trade practices of other countries and could impose trade sanctions against other countries that they believed unfairly restricted US trade. Section 201 of this act allowed the USTR to impose increased duties on imports if they believed that the volume of imports was a substantial cause of damage or potential damage to US domestic industry. This was the equivalent of Article XIX of the GATT agreement (except now the US could unilaterally impose restrictions based on domestic law rather go through the dispute settlement process at GATT), and the USTR did not need to find evidence of any unfair trade practice. Section 301 of this act allowed the US to impose retaliatory tariffs against foreign countries that 'maintained acts, policies and practices that are unreasonable or discriminatory and burden or restrict U.S. Commerce'. This section is sometimes referred to as the Crowbar Act[106], which the US uses as a diplomatic tactic to pressure countries to open their economies to US companies.

As developing economies began to grow and export manufactured products, sometimes competing with US based businesses, the US enacted the Omnibus Trade and Competitiveness Act of 1988, and the section referred to as Special 301, with growing emphasis on Intellectual property rights and protection for US-based companies. The shift of focus from manufactured goods to Intellectual property protection was a key strategy of

---

106 http://internationalecon.com/Trade/Tch20/T20-4.php & Lectures by Dr. Roy Nelson, GPE course at Thunderbird School of Global Management

US trade policy and the US tried to protect its dominance of world trade by preventing other nations and companies from essentially rediscovering or creating products and services that mature industries in the US had already done through intellectual property right definitions.

Each year, the USTR identifies countries that in their estimation, deny effective and adequate protection of intellectual property rights of American businesses and places them on a Watch List or a Priority Watch List. Countries on the Priority Watch List can be subjected to trade sanctions and the US uses this again as a diplomatic tool to pressure countries to keep their markets open and protect the profitability of American businesses. India is currently on the Watch List.

Despite the shift in domestic political compulsions, the US remained committed to the multilateral trading system and continued efforts to reform the GATT system to further trade liberalization. US initiatives launched the GATT trade rounds for multilateral trade negotiations.

GATT Trade Rounds

There have been eight rounds in all under the GATT system of multilateral trade negotiations starting from the first round in Geneva, with only 23 attending countries, to the eight round, known as the Uruguay Round, which took eight years to complete with 123 countries participating in the negotiations. It was at the Uruguay Round that negotiations for the new World Trade Organization (WTO) were also concluded — which led to the replacement of GATT by the WTO.

The Initial Rounds — Geneva-Annecy-Torquay-Geneva: the

first round was the Geneva Round in 1947, where GATT was signed into existence. The trade negotiations at Geneva resulted in 45,000 tariff concessions on trade between the 23 attending countries.

The second round of negotiations took place in Annecy, France in 1949, and lasted five months. The negotiations resulted in some 5000 tariff concessions between the 13 attending countries and most were either unilateral or bilateral tariff concessions.

The third round took place in Torquay, UK in 1950, and lasted eight months. 38 countries participated and negotiated 8,700 tariff concessions cutting the 1948 tariff levels by 25%.

The fourth round took place again in Geneva in 1956, where Japan was admitted into the GATT system and 26 countries participated in these negotiations.

The fifth round of negotiations took place again in Geneva in 1960, but is known as the Dillon Round, after the US Secretary of Treasury, who led the talks. Twenty-six countries participated and further tariff rate cuts were negotiated.

The first five rounds of negotiations primarily focused on reducing tariffs on goods and lasted less than a year each. The next round was the first time the negotiations went beyond tariff reductions to encompass a wide range of other international trade-related topics and the rounds began to take longer to conclude. The sixth round took place between 1964 and 1967, and is known as the Kennedy Round.

The Kennedy Round: 62 countries participated in the Kennedy Round and the discussions went beyond the traditional tariff cuts (this time linear or across the board tariff cuts were discussed as opposed to tariff cuts by product), to discuss non-tariff barriers, preferential treatment for developing countries, as well as extending the anti-dumping code of GATT. Up until the Kennedy Round, developing nations hardly participated in GATT negotiation rounds. Most GATT agreements covered manufactured and industrial goods and specifically excluded agricultural and other tropical products that developing countries had. Agriculture was a large part, most times in excess of 50%, of the GDP of developing countries but they could not benefit from the GATT system as agricultural products were not covered by GATT agreements and developed markets protected their domestic food markets and heavily subsidized agriculture. Textiles, which was the other major product exported by developing countries and was heavily controlled, in violation of the original GATT agreements. The creation of UNCTAD, gave voice to the concerns of developing countries and they began to participate more actively in the trade rounds after the Kennedy Round.

A Brief History of Textile Controls

Japan was a major exporter of cotton textiles to the US after the Second World War and by 1955, the US began experiencing a trade deficit in the textile trade. Domestic manufacturers and their lobbies, put significant political pressure on the government to provide relief to this industry. Following the advice of the US Secretary of State to exercise restraint in its textile exports, Japan announced a voluntary restriction of its exports to the US. The Eisenhower Administration and Japan agreed on a five-year plan for voluntary control on Japan's exports to the US, subject to a quota. This agreement on voluntary export restriction, which essentially was a quota, laid the foundation for violation of GATT agreements in the textile industry. As US demand for textiles outstripped the voluntary quota restrictions on Japan, other countries in Asia began to fill the gap.

In 1961, the Nixon Administration requested the GATT Council to convene a working party to arrive at a multilateral solution to the textile issue and this resulted in the conclusion of a Short-Term Arrangement for international trade in cotton textiles and subsequently the Long Term Arrangement in 1961, valid for a period of five-years. These arrangements provided the framework for developed countries to enter into bilateral or unilateral agreements with developing countries for Voluntary Export Restrictions (VER). In 1974, the Multi-Fiber Agreement, which covered manmade fibers as well as wool, in addition to cotton textiles, went into effect, placing most of the exports from developing countries, other than basic minerals and commodities, under control. The Multi-Fiber agreement would be enhanced in the Uruguay Round and finally ended in 2004, when all restrictions on textile exports were removed.

UNCTAD: another important event that happened during this time was the formation of UNCTAD (United Nations Council for Trade and Development), under the United Nations in 1964. An important economist and thinker that influenced the strategy and direction of many emerging economies, was Raul Prebisch, an Argentinean, who showed that the terms of trade weighed heavily against commodity and raw material exporting countries. He showed that most developing countries were disadvantaged in the global economy as prices for manufactured goods kept on rising relative to primary and commodity goods, which meant developing countries had to export more primary goods every year to import the same amount of manufactured goods. His efforts led to the creation of UNCTAD, and he was appointed as its first Secretary-General.

Developing countries, under the auspices of the UN, established UNCTAD (United Nations Conference on Trade and Development), in 1964, with the goal of helping developing countries integrate into the world economy. It is the main organ of the UN dealing with trade, investment and development issues. Its goals are to maximize the trade, investment and development opportunities of developing countries and assist them in their efforts to integrate into the world economy.

One of the principal achievements of UNCTAD has been to conceive and implement the Generalized System of Preferences (GSP), under which developed nations would agree to import manufactured and some agricultural goods from developing countries duty-free or at a lower tariff than imports from other MFN (other contracting parties in GATT – typically other developed nations), trading partners. The idea was that this would encourage more exports from developing countries and hasten their integration into world trade. In 1971, GATT contracting parties approved a waiver to Article I for 10 years and authorized the GSP Scheme. In 1979, it created a permanent waiver to the most-favored-nation (MFN) clause, to allow preferential treatment for developing and least developed countries.

The Rise of Non-Tariff Barriers (NTBs): as worldwide competition grew for manufactured goods and the once export surplus US economy turned current account negative, many vulnerable industries began lobbying the government for support and protection. As most developed countries had agreed to reduce tariffs under GATT negotiations, the only viable option left to protect domestic industry was the so called Non-Tariff Barriers. These included subsidies and tax preferences to help ailing industries, incentives to develop new technology and R&D, requirement for local content, government procurement policies, customs procedures, national standards, and a number of other ingenuous rules embedded in national economic and industrial policies.

These non-tariff measures had trade distorting consequences and soon threatened to negate what had been achieved through GATT tariff reducing agreements and liberalization of the global economy. The other principal barrier was the proliferation of Voluntary Export restrictions (as discussed in the case of textiles). Steel was the other major industry that implemented VERs among developed economies, when the US negotiated VREs with the EU and Japan in 1968. Another industry subjected to VERs was the automobile industry, when Britain, France and the US negotiated VERs with Japan to restrict the export of automobiles. In the face of these new protections and non-tariff barriers, the GATT system became increasingly out of place and irrelevant. Developing countries such as Brazil and India wanted agricultural products to be covered by GATT and the agenda for the next round of talks was based on these issues of non-tariff barriers, VERs and agriculture.

The Tokyo Round: the seventh round of GATT trade negotiations from 1973 to 1979, is referred to as the Tokyo Round and for the first time, agricultural issues was on the agenda in addition to dealing with non-tariff barriers and VERs. The Tokyo Round began in the middle of an oil crisis and a deep recession worldwide, as well as being the first time countries were negotiating under the new flexible exchange rate system. While no significant change in policies relating to agricultural products was achieved, the most important outcome of the Tokyo Round was made with respect to non-tariff barriers[107]. A new code on subsidies and countervailing duties was created to deal with national industrial policies recognizing subsidies as non-tariff barriers and allowed members to retaliate with import tariff increases (countervailing duties), to compensate for subsidies. A dumping code established comparable rules for anti-dumping measures.

The code on government procurement recognized government purchasing policies as non-tariff barriers and set rules for equal treatment for both national and foreign firms bidding for government contracts. Other codes, covering product standards and customs valuation, established rules for dealing with these kinds of non-tariff barriers.

Despite these successes, there were a number of unresolved issues such as VERs and agricultural products. The Multi-Fiber Agreement was renewed for another five-year term. Trade conflicts became more frequent and more heated. As the dispute resolution mechanism was weak, a number of these codes on non-tariff barriers increased frustration with the system. Additionally, there were a number of other developments in the global economy. Trade in services was becoming an increasingly larger part of international trade and began to play a bigger role in the domestic GDP. The nature of business was also shifting from

---

107 A number of these agreements were signed only by a few of the Contracting Parties and not by all members – hence they are referred to as codes and only obliged those that ratified them to comply with the provisions.

simple goods to more sophisticated products incorporating advanced technologies and a corresponding demand from industry to protect intellectual property rights. GATT, which was designed to cover primarily manufactured goods, needed to be upgraded massively to deal with all these issues.

During this time (1973-79), some developing countries began to move into manufacturing and exports and started to participate in negotiations at GATT. But most were still eligible for preferences and preferred to work under VERs. India's concerns at this time were primarily about agricultural products and VERs in the textile industry.

The Uruguay Round: two years after the end of the Tokyo Round, the US initiated a process towards launching a new round of talks. It wanted to initiate discussions on agreements in new areas such as Services, Intellectual Property Rights and Investments, and to include them as a part of GATT. In 1982, GATT held a ministerial meeting to decide on a new round of talks and to come up with the agenda for the round. A number of developing countries, led by India and Brazil, opposed the extension of GATT into these new areas and instead called for completing the negotiations on Agriculture, VERs and other items of importance to them. Though the 1982 meeting was unsuccessful in meeting its objectives, pre-negotiations to the Uruguay Round continued. India and Brazil, along with Argentina, Egypt, Yugoslavia, Cuba, Nigeria, Nicaragua, Peru and Tanzania, formed a group of 10 countries opposing new rounds of talks who were completely opposed to including new issues such as services within the purview of GATT[108].

---

108 *Development, Trade and the WTO: a handbook*, Issue 2 by Bernand M. Hoekman, Aaditya Mattoo & Philip English

The US was adamant about including the new topics of Services, Intellectual Property Rights and others, and issued an ultimatum that if those topics were not on the agenda, it would withdraw from the conference altogether and unilaterally impose import restrictions under sections 301[109].

The G9 group (9 wealthiest countries), presented an alternate proposal and secured support from another set of developing countries who formed the *Café au Lait* group[110], including Bangladesh, Chile, Colombia, Cote d'Ivore, Hong Kong, Indonesia, Jamaica, Korea, Malaysia, Mexico, Pakistan, Philippines, Romania, Singapore, Sri Lanka, Thailand, Turkey, Uruguay, Zambia and Zaire. This coalition won out and the final agenda for the next round of discussions included all the new topics that the US wanted though the original group of 10 opposing members did not go empty-handed as the issues of Agriculture, VERs and the Multi-Fiber Agreement, were also included for negotiations. India, Brazil and the US also came to an agreement that negotiations on services would be undertaken separately and not tied to the ongoing negotiations for products. In the following negotiations in Punta Del Esta, the US, India and Brazil were the principal participants on a numbers of subjects.

The Uruguay Round of multilateral trade negotiations was finally formally launched in September 1986 at Punta Del Este, Uruguay almost five years later than originally planned and included a broad agenda. The negotiations lasted seven and a half years – almost twice the original schedule, with 123 countries taking part[111]. It

---

109 'Rediscovering the Role of Developing Countries in GATT before the Doha Round', Faizel Ismail, RIS-DP #141, http://www.ris.org.in/dp141_pap.pdf
110 See 69
111 http://www.wto.org/English/thewto_e/whatis_e/tif_e/fact5_e.htm

was the most ambitious trade negotiation ever undertaken and covered almost every aspect of international trade. In the last two years of the negotiations, Canada introduced a new proposal to create a new institution which it called the World Trade Organization. When the final deal was signed on 15 April 1994, by ministers from most of the 123 participating governments, at a meeting in Marrakesh, it included significant new agreements on a number of issues, as well as the birth of the new organization to oversee and enforce their implementation. The WTO was born.

In addition to traditional GATT issues such as tariff reductions, the Uruguay Round accomplished a number of significant changes and agreements including a major revamping of the Dispute Settlement Mechanism; an agreement to phase out the Multi-Fiber Agreement by 2004; an agreement on Trade-related aspects of Intellectual Property Rights (TRIPS); an agreement on Trade-related Investment Measures (TRIMs); and a new General Agreement on Trade in Services (GATS). Some progress was made on discussions related to agricultural products but this is one area where significant changes have yet to be seen.

IMPACT OF GATT ON WORLD TRADE

GATT has had a significant impact on world trade which has grown substantially since it came into force. The volume of world trade grew at an unprecedented average rate of 8% annually between the founding of GATT in 1947 and the first oil shock in 1973. Although the annual rate declined during the period between the two oil shocks, it recovered to 6.5% during the period 1990-99. Trade growth has exceeded the growth rate of world output every year since 1950 and trade has grown 15 times its level in 1950, as compared to output, which grew only six times[112]. India, however, did not enjoy the benefits of this growing world trade and her share of world trade actually declined from more than 2% in the early 1950s to about 0.7% in 2000.[113]

Up until 1991, India had a closed economy and development policies were centrally planned and inward looking, made in the Five-Year Plans by the Planning Commission. India particularly resorted to Article XVIII of the GATT agreements, which allowed developing countries to restrict imports based on (Section B) balance-of-payments issues and imposed Quantitative Restrictions (QRs) on imports. Also, India's economy was primarily agriculture-based and GATT did not include any agricultural products in its scope and the other export item, textiles, was controlled by VERs.

The quantitative restrictions were challenged by the US and others and the dispute settlement board ruled against India. India finally removed all its QRs in 2000 and 2001[114]. Import tariffs also began their downward climb only after reforms and the liberalization process was begun in 1991. The Peak rate came down from 150% in 1991-92 to about 20% at the end of 2003-04[115]. India's trade with the world has also substantially increased since liberalization and in 2009, the WTO estimated India's share of world trade at 2.8% or the ninth largest[116] in the world – a significant turnaround from the late '80s.

---

112 http://www.piie.com/publications/chapters_preview/98/3iie2806.pdf
113 See 79
114 http://www.icrier.org/pdf/WP172.pdf
115 http://www.icrier.org/pdf/WP172.pdf
116 http://www.wto.org/english/news_e/pres09_e/pr554_e.htm

THE WTO

One of the most dramatic results of the Uruguay Round has been the establishment of the WTO to replace GATT. The Marrakesh agreement gave legal sanction to the establishment of the WTO as a fully fledged legal international organization. The rules and decisions made at the WTO are now binding on its members. The agreement establishing the World Trade Organization is informally referred to as the WTO Charter and the substantive treaty obligation texts are appended in 4 annexes as follows.

Annex 1 contains all the trade agreements including all the GATT agreements as well as the new agreements on services, intellectual property rights and investments agreed until and at the Uruguay Round. The tariff schedules are also part of this annex.

Annex 2 contains the dispute settlement rules and these are obligatory for all members. The dispute settlement process at WTO has been vastly improved over the GATT process, including strict timeframes and adoption through what is called the reverse consensus process (i.e. all members must vote to overturn a ruling of the dispute panel otherwise those rulings are adopted and are binding).

Annex 3 contains the Trade Policy Review Mechanism (TPRM), by which WTO reviews overall trade policies of each member on a periodic basis.

Annex 4 contains four agreements that are optional and also known as plurilateral agreements.

WTO has nearly 150[117] members, accounting for over 97% of world trade. The organizational structure consists of the Ministerial Conference, the top level decision-making body and meets at least every two years. Decisions are made by consensus, by the entire membership. Below the Ministerial Conference is the General Council, which meets several times a year in the Geneva headquarters and is also the dispute settlement body. At the next level are the different councils such as the Goods Council, Services Council etc, who report to the General Council. WTO also has a Secretariat based in Geneva, whose primary duties are to supply technical reports for the various councils, committees and conferences. The Secretariat also provides some forms of legal assistance in the dispute settlement process and advises governments wishing to become members. The Director-General of WTO supervises the WTO Secretariat and is appointed by WTO members for a term of four years. The Director-General has little power over matters of policy as the organization's decisions are made by member States through the Ministerial Conferences.

The WTO is not a part of the UN nor is it a specialized agency of the UN – though it does work closely with the IMF and World Bank.

Dispute Settlement at the WTO (Annex 2): significant changes have been made to the dispute settlement process at WTO as compared what it was under GATT –which has made it much more effective. This is now based on clearly defined rules with timetables for completing a case. An appeal against the panel ruling can be made once and is reviewed by an Appellate Board. Once the ruling has been

---

117 http://www.wto.org/english/thewto_e/whatis_e/inbrief_e/inbr02_e.htm

confirmed, modified or denied by the Appellate Board, it comes into effect and can only be overturned by reverse consensus (every member has to agree to overturn the panel decision), which (almost) never happens.

A dispute arises when one country adopts a trade policy or takes an action that other members of the WTO consider to be breaking WTO agreements. A country can then initiate a dispute settlement process and other members may join as third party members in the process. The Dispute Settlement body has the sole authority to establish panels of experts to consider a case and has the power to authorize retaliation by the plaintiff (and third parties to the case). WTO does not itself initiate any retaliatory action and panel rulings are enforced by the members themselves under the authorization given by WTO. A fixed timeline has been specified[118] and the process should take no longer than a year without an appeal or a year and three months with an appeal.

These changes have made the process more effective and the Dispute Settlement Panel at WTO has seen members raise issues at two or three times the rate under GATT. The Dispute Settlement process is the same for all agreements in WTO, including the new agreements on services (GATS), intellectual property rights (TRIPs) and investments (TRIMs).

A number of cases have come before the Dispute Settlement Panel since WTO came into effect. India, along with a few other Asian countries, brought a dispute over the US ban on shrimp imports to the Dispute Panel in 1997, and the Panel ruled in their favour. In response to President

---

118 http://www.wto.org/English/thewto_e/whatis_e/tif_e/disp1_e.htm

Bush's invocation of Section 301 (of the US Trade Act 1974), to protect the domestic US steel industry, the EU and Japan, challenged this unilateral action at the WTO Dispute Panel and got a ruling in their favour – which forced the US to withdraw protection.

An interesting case from the perspective of developing nations and agricultural exports, is the one Brazil brought against the US for subsidizing domestic cotton farming as well as its export in 2002 (dispute settlement case DS267), against specific provisions of the US cotton program. The US is the third largest producer of cotton in the world (behind China and India), and the world's largest exporter at almost 37% of world trade[119]. A number of domestic subsidies that include direct payments, counter-cyclical program payments, marketing loan benefits, Step 2 payments and others, are available to cotton growers and exporters, valued at an average of $3.5 Billion per year. Brazil successfully argued that these subsidies go against WTO agreements and contributed to significant over-production which resulted in a surge of US cotton exports, particularly during 1999-2002 and that this substantially affected Brazilian exports of cotton and caused a steep decline in world cotton prices. Brazil estimated the financial impact to its economy due to these US subsidies for cotton, at over $600 million in the year 2001 alone.

In 2004, the WTO Dispute Settlement Panel ruled in favour of Brazil and later in 2005, an appellate body reviewing the initial ruling and upheld the original panel's decision. The US made several changes to its cotton programs to bring them into compliance with WTO recommendations but Brazil argued that the US response was inadequate and

---

119 http://www.nationalaglawcenter.org/assets/crs/RL32571.pdf

requested the establishment of a WTO compliance panel in 2006 to review US actions. The compliance panel ruled against the US in 2007 and it was upheld by an appellate panel in 2008. On 21 December 2009, Brazil announced that it was authorized by the WTO to impose trade retaliation against the US imports for up to $829.3 Million and in 2010, released a final list of goods of US origin that would be subject to import tariffs. This case highlights the growing confidence of developing nations in challenging the actions of the developed and powerful countries and the growing importance of multilateral organizations such as WTO, in enforcing agreed upon rules equitably.

GATS (PART OF ANNEX 1)

The General Agreement on Trade in Services (GATS), was negotiated at the Uruguay Round and came into force in January 1995, under WTO, almost 50 years after its counterpart, GATT, came into effect. Service businesses include hotels and restaurants, professional services such as medicine, law and teaching, utilities such as electricity, water and transportation and other activities that do not involve the transfer of a physical product.

The need for a trade agreement in services has been (and continues to be), questioned by many (the reason being that it is 50 years behind GATT), as most of these have traditionally been considered either domestic businesses or the responsibility of the local government (or government-owned monopolies). But the tremendous growth of world trade in products as well as the rapid development of new technologies, has reopened the need for an international agreement in the services industry. As people travelled across the world more, either for vacation or business, they began to look for and support known brands of hotel chains and restaurants, opening up business possibilities for homegrown brands to expand internationally. Similarly, the need for money exchange, banking and other financial services, necessitated the presence of international banks and financial institutions around the world.

The rapidly changing telecommunications and internet technologies have allowed remote customer servicing and has opened up opportunities for outsourcing and other service industries. In addition, a number of governments have broken up their traditional monopolies in utilities, transportation and other services, as part of their liberalization programs and allowed competition in these industries – opening up new avenues for private (both domestic and international) participation in these sectors. Services has become the most dynamic and fast-growing segment of domestic economies as well as international trade and an international system was needed to help it to grow unhindered.

Similar to GATT, GATS is intended to contribute to service trade expansion 'under conditions of transparency and progressive liberalization as a means of promoting the economic growth of all trading partners and the development of developing countries[120]'. Terms like MFN (Most Favored Nation) and National Treatment, have been taken from the GATT agreement and incorporated into GATS. The concept of progressive liberalization, which requires members to meet regularly and forge new agreements, is also familiar to all members of GATT.

Unlike GATT, however, individual governments have the right (called Scheduling), to specify which sectors

---

120 http://www.wto.org/english/tratop_e/serv_e/cbt_course_e/c1s2p1_e.htm

and under what conditions, these sectors will be open to international trade. They can evaluate and introduce new regulations if required to meet national policy objectives and specific domestic needs. GATT also does not cover services provided to the public in the exercise of governmental authority and in the air transport sector.

For the purpose of the agreement, the definition of services trade has been classified into 12 sectors and having four modes. The 12 sectors of services trade are:

1. Business services including professional and computer services
2. Communication services
3. Construction and Engineering services,
4. Distribution services including wholesale and retail
5. Education services
6. Environment service
7. Finance including insurance and banking,
8. Health Services
9. Tourism and Travel services
10. Recreation, Cultural and Sporting services
11. Transportation services
12. Everything else not classified above.

The four modes of service delivery include:

Mode 1 A service that is delivered from the territory of one member into the territory of another member or called cross-border trade. Examples include all outsourcing activity done in the home country (i.e. no one has travelled but the service has been accomplished through communication technologies). This is important to India as the preferred outsourcing destination in the world and further liberalization of this mode across different sectors will help boost India's (services) export revenue.

Mode 2 A service that is delivered in the territory of one member to the consumer of any other members, also called 'consumption abroad'. Examples include tourists from one country going to another country and consuming hotel, restaurant and tourism services. This mode is becoming increasingly important from India's point of view, for services like healthcare outsourcing, where patients from developed countries come to India for medical services that cost far less than in their countries, with comparable safety and quality. If insurance coverage in developed countries accepts medical outsourcing as a legitimate medical expense covered under their policies, this industry has the potential to grow tremendously in India and offers a real chance of reducing healthcare costs in developed countries.

Mode 3 A service that is delivered by a member through their commercial presence in the territory of another member, also called 'commercial presence'. Examples include banks of one member establishing a physical commercial presence in another country. In this case, the service supplier establishes a legal presence in the form of a joint venture, subsidiary or a branch office in the host country and services customers there. This mode is of particular importance for multinational companies as they set up their offices worldwide.

Mode 4 A service that is delivered by the physical presence of a natural person of one member in the territory of any other member, also known as 'presence of natural persons'. Examples include Indian IT consultants working on projects abroad, Indonesian and Philippino maids in Singapore and other rich nations in Asia etc. This mode is also of importance to India given the growth of the IT consulting industry and the need at times for engineers to be physically present at client sites. Most developed countries restrict the movement of people through work permit regulations and quotas and it is in India's interest to push for a WTO or GATT visa that can bypass these non-tariff barriers to the services trade.

COUNTRY SCHEDULES

Article XX of the GATS agreements sets out the rules regarding country-specific Schedules that they undertake to open up for international participation. In the Schedule, each member sets out the specific commitments it undertakes with respect to sectors and the conditions for other GATS members which include:

    a. terms, limitations and conditions on market access
    b. conditions and qualifications on national treatment
    c. undertakings relating to additional commitments
    d. a time frame implementation of such commitments
    e. the date of entry into force of such commitments.

Members can set two types of conditions in their schedules: Horizontal commitments which apply to all sectors and Sector Specific Commitments for specific sectors including:

    a. limitations on the number of service suppliers
    b. limitations on the total value of services transactions or assets
    c. limitations on the total number of service operations or the total quantity of service output
    d. limitations of the number of persons that may be

       employed in a particular sector or by a particular supplier

  e. measures that restrict or require specific types of legal entity or joint ventures and

  f. limitations on the participation of foreign capital or on the total value of foreign investment. This allows individual members flexibility and a well defined transparent mechanism to implement liberalization or service sectors based on their country priorities and needs.

India submitted its original Schedule of specific commitments in April 1994[121]. This contained Horizontal commitments such as conditions on Business Visitors and preferential access to suppliers with the best terms for transfer of technology. Sector Specific commitments included opening up of the Business Services segment, including computer-related and consultancy services; research and development services excluding atomic research; telecommunications services with a restriction on a foreign equity ceiling of 51%; motion picture and video distribution services with a restriction of 100 titles a year; construction work for civil engineering with a restriction of foreign equity ceiling of 51%; non-life insurance related services; banking services with restrictions on number of licenses per year initially at five and with other restrictions on capital requirement; and sectors such as health and tourism.

As members negotiate with others and agree on new conditions, supplements to the original Schedule are submitted to WTO. India has made a number of such

---

121   http://commerce.nic.in/trade/international_trade_matters_service_
indianpapers_generalagreement_5.asp

supplements to the original Schedule, including Supplement 1 and 2 in 1995, Supplement 3 in 1997 and so on[122].

NEGOTIATIONS UNDER GATS

Negotiating principles under GATS are contained in the Guidelines and Procedures for Negotiations on Trade in Services or NGP (Negotiating Guidelines and Procedures), which India along with 22 other developing members, played a significant role in its preparation and adoption. The main elements of NGP are:

a. a commitment to progressive liberalization with due respect to national policy objectives, the level of development and the size of economies
b. maintaining the existing structure and principle of GATS including Schedules and the right to choose the sectors and modes of supply while undertaking commitments
c. the Request-Offer approach as the main method of negotiations
d. a goal of increasing the participation of developing countries in the Trade in Services.

The Request-Offer approach involves members setting out their Offers (concessions that they are willing to offer in giving greater market access to import of services), based on their current Schedules as well as their Requests (their list of demands seeking greater market access for the export of their services), and negotiating with other members either bilaterally or multilaterally. Commitments agreed to during this process then become part of the members' obligations under GATS.

___

122 Details of all the supplements can be found on Ministry of Commerce, Government of India's, website at: http://commerce.nic.in/trade/international_trade_matters_service_indianpapers_generalagreement.asp

India made its Conditional Initial Offer in January 2004[123], as part of this Request-Offer approach to negotiations. Among the offers are: increasing the limits on foreign equity ceiling to 74% in computer-related services and medical services; further liberalizations in the telecom sector; increasing the number of licenses in the banking sector to 15; and opening up of private sector banks in India to FDI with a ceiling of 49%; further liberalization in financial services including stock broking and venture capital; and opening of up the maritime transport services industry (the reason why India now have access to Cruise Lines). A revised offer was also made in August 2005[124].

India's requests are primarily in the further opening up of international markets under Mode 1 (Cross Border supply) and Mode 4 (Movement of Natural Persons), of the modes of service and India has been seeking broad based commitments in key sectors such as IT and off-shoring of services. India has a large pool of well qualified professionals in a number of service sectors and a large comparative advantage over other members of GATS and it is in her best interests to further liberalize these modes of services delivery.

To further promote liberalization of Mode 4, India submitted a proposal on Liberalization of Movement of Professionals (S/CSS/W/12) in November 2000. In particular the proposal highlights the various measures taken by developed member countries in restricting Mode 4 services by measures such as the Economic Needs Test, restrictive visa regimes, non-recognition of educational and technical qualifications and others. It also provides strategies for

---

123 http://commerce.nic.in/trade/initial_offer1.pdf
124 http://commerce.nic.in/trade/revised_offer1.pdf

improving access such as transparency in visa regimes, creation of a separate GATS visa which is less onerous than the normal immigration visa and facilitation of Mutual Recognition Agreements.

IMPACT OF GATS ON INDIA

The growth of the services industry in India has transformed its economy and now contributes to more than 50% of India's GDP. The services industry is the fastest growing segment in India, contributing to almost three-fourths[125] of the growth of India's GDP. This growing importance of the Service industry to India's overall growth has accelerated India's participation in GATS and since the Doha Ministerial Meetings in 2001, India has emerged as a leading proponent of services trade liberalization under GATS. Liberalization of service sectors such as IT, Telecommunications, Hotels, Banking and Finance, has led to the tremendous growth of these industries in India.

The phenomenal growth of telecommunications as an industry segment, is a great example – where the number of cellular phones has grown from virtually being non-existent to more than 600 Million, making India one of the world's largest and fastest growing markets. According to the Economic Survey 2009-10, services exports reached US $102 Billion in 2008-09, registering a growth of 12.5% over 2007-08 (in a year of recession around the world), making India the ninth ranked exported of commercial services.

The growth of IT and software services has contributed significantly to this growth and contributes 45.5% of the overall export of services[126]. Without a doubt,

---

125 http://www.thomex.com/article/resources_details.aspx?ID=R_200706041 4180&catid=C_20071024132144&flag=0
126 http://www.ibef.org/economy/services.aspx

India has benefitted from liberalizing its services industry and continues to be an active proponent of GATS for further commitments and liberalization of its service sectors.

Economic reforms are taking place in many sectors of the services economy in India, including financial services, telecommunications, education services, health services and professional services. An example is the IRDA Act of 1999 (Insurance Regulatory and Development Authority), which opened up the insurance sector to foreign equity participation with a ceiling of 26%. The FDI limit in the telecommunications sector has been raised to 74% of the total equity. The government has also passed or is considering, legislation to open up other sectors such as education and the postal services, among others. A number of these reforms are being done at a pace the government deems appropriate – such as opening up FDI in the retail industry only for Single Brand retail, though there have been calls for opening up Multi Brand retail by industry giants such as Wal-Mart. While India has benefitted under GATS, not every country or group of industries and individuals around the world are convinced about the positive impact of GATS and there have been some criticisms levied against it.

Criticism of GATS

The primary criticism of GATS is against the intrusion of private industry into sectors traditionally under the domain of government services, such as health services. Critics contend that under the Progressive Liberalization mandate of GATS, critical service sectors will be forced to open up to private competition and general public services such as health and water and sanitation will be diverted by private corporations to those who can afford to pay while neglecting the poor and weaker sections of society.

A global campaign to stop GATS, known as GATSwatch, was launched in 2001 and its main points of critique[127] are:

a. negative impacts on universal access to basic services such as healthcare, education, water and transport
b. fundamental conflict between freeing up trade in services and the right of governments and communities to regulate companies in areas such as tourism, retail, telecommunications and broadcasting
c. absence of comprehensive assessment of the impact of GATS-style liberalization before further negotiations continue
d. a one-sided deal in favour of developed nations.

GATS is primarily about expanding opportunities for large multinational companies. The organization ActionAid[128] has argued that expecting governments to have the required knowledge to list all potentially GATS incompatible regulations is unrealistic for the poorest countries. They have also criticized the current Offer-Request mode of negotiations under GATS, claiming that the bilateral and secretive approach enables the powerful countries to put huge pressure on developing countries to remove restrictions for their trans-national corporations.

One particular sector that is the cause of great concern is water, specifically water supply. Many critics argue that water is a basic right of all people and allowing private corporations to control water supply will increase

127 http://www.gatswatch.org/
128 http://www.actionaid.org/docs/general_agreement_trade_services.pdf

the cost of water well beyond the paying capacity of many of the poorest people in developing and under-developed countries. A related issue in the Indian context is the criticism against Coca-Cola in the Indian state of Kerala. Critics contend that Coca-Cola's bottling plant is depleting the watertable at an alarming rate to enable the production of soft drinks. These drinks are targeted at the economically well-to-do sections of society. The poor who live close to the plant, depend on access to the same water source through wells, for agriculture as well as their daily needs. They are severely affected by the declining watertable and bear the brunt of the investment. This redistribution of natural resources away from the poor to the rich by private enterprise, is by far the most critical consequence of development and globalization. Developing countries must contemplate and implement national policies to protect their citizens while participating in the global growth of the services industry to grow their economies and lift their people out of poverty.

TRIPS (PART OF ANNEX 1)

The WTO agreement on Trade Related Aspects of Intellectual Property Rights (TRIPS) was also negotiated during the Uruguay Round and brought intellectual property rules for the first time into the set of rules and agreements on global trade.

Intellectual property rights are those given to persons and companies for the creations they make, invent or design. These rights give the creator exclusive use of the creation for a certain period of time, including the authority to license it to others. Intellectual property rights are traditionally divided into two areas:

1. Copyright and rights related to copyright which includes those such as the right of authors of literary and artistic works given for a minimum period of fifty-years after the death of the author.
2. Industrial property rights which includes both trademarks and other distinctive signs of a company and patents which protect innovation, design and the creation of new technology and/ or products and services.

Intellectual property rights protect the right of the creators over their works and encourage and rewards creative work. Patents protect the investment made into the development of new technology, giving the incentive and the means to finance new research and development activities and are typically given for 20 years[129].

Protection of intellectual property is not new. The Paris Convention for the Protection of Industrial Property in 1883, and the Berne Convention in 1886 for the Protection of Literary and Artistic Works, set international agreements governing intellectual property rights and had elements of the concepts of MFN and National Treatment in them. In 1893, the bureau set up to handle administrative tasks for both the Paris and Berne Conventions, merged to become the United International Bureaux for the Protection of Intellectual Property and in 1967, became the World Intellectual Property Organization (WIPO). In 1974. it became an organization within the United Nations. As we have seen before, the US does not particularly like to deal through the UN as it is deemed too cumbersome and ineffective and the US does not have special voting rights or privileges to enforce its view.

---

129 http://www.wto.org/english/tratop_e/trips_e/intel1_e.htm

The US pushed for the inclusion of intellectual property rights through the WTO agreements which led to the adoption of the TRIPS Agreement during the Uruguay Round. Through the TRIPS Agreement, on the foundations built by WIPO, members of the WTO attempted to narrow the gaps in the way intellectual property rights are protected around the world and established a set of common international rules to protect and promote new research and creativity. These agreements established the minimum level of protection each member government has to give to the intellectual property of other members. The agreement covers the following broad issues:

a. how to give adequate protection to intellectual property rights
b. how countries should enforce those rights in their countries
c. how to settle disputes
d. special transitional agreements during the adjustment period.

The TRIPS agreement is the most comprehensive agreement on intellectual property rights and deals with all types of Intellectual property rights with the sole exception of breeders' rights. Intellectual property rights covered under TRIPS include:

1. Copyright and related rights
2. Trademarks
3. Geographical indications
4. Industrial designs
5. Patents
6. Layout designs of Integrated Circuits
7. Protection of trade secrets

Copyright: in addition to the rights as agreed to at the Berne Convention, the TRIPS agreement included computer programs as well as rental rights to producers of sound recordings and films. The rights include the rights of reproduction, communication to the public, adaptation and the translation of the work.

Trademarks: a trademark is a distinctive sign which identifies certain goods or services as produced by a specific person or company. Trademarks help consumers identify and purchase a product or service that they have come to identify with as satisfying their needs. The TRIPS agreement defines what types of signs are eligible for protection as trademarks and the minimum rights conferred on their owners.

Geographical Indications: a place name is sometimes used to identify a product including its special characteristics which as the result of the product's origins, such as Champagne. TRIPS agreement contains special provision to protect the IP of such products.

Industrial Design: under the TRIPS agreement, industrial designs must be protected for at least 10 years and owners must be able to prevent the manufacture, sale or importation of articles bearing and using a design that has been given a copyright by member countries.

Patents: under the TRIPS agreement, members must provide patent protection for inventions of both products and processes for at least 20 years. This has caused significant debate about product patents for medicines which make them expensive and out of reach for many people in developing and least-developed countries. There is a safeguard built in called Compulsory Licenses, which a government can issue to allow competitors to produce the product or use the process under license to provide sufficient quantity of the product for the domestic market.

Integrated Circuits & Layouts: the TRIPS agreement is based on the Washington Treaty on intellectual Property in Respect of Integrated Circuits under WIPO, and member countries must provide protection for a minimum of 10 years.

Trade Secrets: the TRIPS agreement requires member countries to keep trade secrets revealed to the local government for the approval of certain products such as pharmaceutical or agricultural chemicals confidential and protect submitting companies from unfair commercial use of such information.

The TRIPS agreement shares the basic principles of other WTO agreements like MFN (Most Favored Nation) and National Treatment clauses. It also recognized the special needs of the least-developed country members in respect of providing flexibility in the implementation of laws and regulations.

Enforcement of the agreement is covered in Part 3 of TRIPS and requires governments have sufficient legislations that allow them to enforce the agreement under their laws. The agreement also covers dispute settlement and members must follow WTO's dispute settlement procedures to resolve disputes related to intellectual property rights. With respect to developing economies and the flexibility given to them in implementing TRIPS, developing countries were allowed until 2000, to apply the provisions of the agreement and least-developed countries were given until 2006 (later extended until 2016 for certain products such as pharmaceuticals), to implement the provisions.

IMPACT OF TRIPS ON PHARMACEUTICALS & INDIA

Prior to modifying its patent laws in 2005, the laws on intellectual property protection with respect to patents in India were governed by the Patents Act 1970[130]. Section 5 in chapter 2 of this Act, specifically allowed for only what are called 'process patents' in case of inventions of substances intended for use or capable of being used as food or as medicine or drugs and for substance prepared or produced by chemical processes including alloys, optical glass, semi-conductors and inter-metallic compounds. Patents were not granted for the product itself but claims for the methods or processes of manufacture, were patentable.

This was one of the reasons for the rapid growth of the pharmaceutical industry in India and specifically in generic drugs and came to be regarded by UNCTAD as a model for developing countries. As product patents were not recognized in India, many companies in India invented new ways of manufacturing both new and patented-in-the-US-and-elsewhere drugs, and made them available for a fraction of their cost, in the domestic market and began to export them to other least-developed countries (LDCs) facing critical medical crises such as the AIDS epidemic. A year's worth of AZT therapy could be bought in India for $500 compared to $5000–$10000 from multinational companies that held product patents. India manufactures and exports more than half the medicines currently used for AIDS treatments in the developing world and over 80% of the 80,000 AIDS patients in Doctors Without Borders projects[131].

---

130 http://ipindia.nic.in/ipr/patent/patents.htm
131 http://ipsnews.net/news.asp?idnews=38840

Many criticized TRIPS as a way for developed countries and their multinational pharmaceutical industries to protect their profit at the cost of many lives in developing and the least-developed countries. South Africa, which faced the brunt of the HIV/AIDS epidemic with almost 20% of its population suffering from the disease, sought to ease the financial strain of patented drugs and enacted the Medicines and Related Substance Control Bill in 1997, which allowed the importation of Indian drugs (through a provision in TRIPS called 'parallel imports'), at almost a tenth of the cost of similar drugs from the US and Europe. 39 drug companies brought suit against the South African government and the US government put immense pressure to prevent the passage of this bill to protect its industry's profit. The international AIDS conference in Durban in 2000, put the spotlight on the issue of affordability of essential medicines for epidemics such as HIV/AIDS. After intense campaigning by AIDS and health activists (some targeted directly at Presidential candidate Al Gore, for his support of the US pharmaceutical industry), the US retreated from its position and eventually reached a resolution with South Africa in 2001.

At the WTO's Ministerial Conference in 2001, India and other developing countries led the Doha Declaration on the TRIPs Agreement and Public Health and it was adopted in response to the protests. The resolution recognized the right of member governments to grant compulsory licenses to local drug producers to make drugs needed in emergency situations. In 2002, a measure to give least-developed countries time until 2016, to protect pharmaceutical patents, was adopted. In 2003, a resolution to remove limitations on exports under compulsory license to countries that cannot manufacture pharmaceuticals themselves, was removed.

These steps helped make it easier for developing and least-developed countries to cope with their basic health and wellbeing necessities.

In 2005, India enacted the Patents (Amendment) Act of 2005[132], which removed Section 5 from the Patent Act of 1970 (removed limitation on patentability to processes only), and made India's patent laws compliant with the requirements under TRIPS. Nevertheless, the issue is complex and controversies over patent rights for drugs and other essential products continue in different countries around the world. Novartis, the Swiss pharmaceutical giant, took the Indian government to court demanding patent protection for its *Gleevec* cancer medication. India had denied the patent based on a clause in India's patent laws that grants protection only for 'real innovations'. Novartis was seeking a patent for modifications to a molecule it had previously invented in order to extend its monopoly on existing drugs for cancer treatment. Novartis prices its brand (*Gleevec*) at $3000 per dose, while Indian generic drug manufacturers sell it at $200.

Given that the per capita income in India is only $1000, the Novartis price puts it out of reach for many Indian patients. More than half of million people signed a petition distributed by Doctors Without Borders, calling on Novartis to drop the case. The Chennai High Court, in a landmark decision in 2007, upheld India's Patents Act and dismissed the petition by Novartis. Similar stories are playing out in other countries as well.

In 2007, the US and EU governments protested against Thailand's efforts to provide generic versions of

---

132 http://ipindia.nic.in/ipr/patent/patent_2005.pdf

Plavix (a drug for heart disease), to millions of poor patients in Thailand.

Cost of TRIPS – India Changes its Laws to Comply

Another criticism of TRIPS is the cost of compliance. Many countries have had to substantially revise their intellectual property laws and invest in the enforcement of them at substantial cost to their government and economy without realizing much or any benefit from TRIPS to their economies. India has had to amend several laws to be in compliance or be on a path to compliance with TRIPS. The Copyright Act of 1957, has been amended five times in 1983, 1984, 1992, 1994 and 1999, with the amendment made in 1994, being the most substantial.

India passed the Trade Marks Act 1999, to be compliant with the TRIPS agreement on Trade Mark Protection. The Geographical Indications of Goods (Registration and Protection) Act 1999, came into force with effect from September 2003, to be compliant with the geographical indications provisions of TRIPS. The Designs Act 2000 legislation, was passed to conform to the Industrial Designs Agreements in TRIPS. The Patent Act of 2005, as previously discussed, got India in compliance with TRIPS on patent regulations. In addition to updating laws, investments are needed to improve the administration of these laws including physical structures, computerized information systems, new staff and extensive training for existing staff as well as investments required to enforce them.

Experts have estimated that 90% of all royalty payments from Intellectual property licensing rights flow into four advanced nations and the rest have negative trade balances on their TRIPS account. Not much information is available on the benefits accrued to India by agreeing to TRIPS but she has not yet reached the break-even point where revenue garnered through licensing of intellectual property rights by Indian companies exceed the government expenditure on implementing and enforcing TRIPS. Nevertheless, Indian companies and individuals are beginning to register more patents and time will tell if these result into positive cash flows for the country.

OTHER CRITICISMS OF TRIPS

Many critics have said that the focus of TRIPS has not been in encouraging innovation or protecting indigenous technology in developing countries but rather enforcing intellectual property rights on behalf of transnational companies in developed economies to collect royalty payments from developing countries – a cash flow that did not exist before the Uruguay Round. They also argue that intellectual property rights and associated TRIPS rules can be interpreted as a way for developed economies to protect and promote Intellectual Hegemony. Many aspects of the TRIPS agreements have been called in question – such as patent rights to be granted regardless of whether the products are imported or locally produced. This meant that patent holders could merely export their product under the patent monopoly instead of transferring technology or making foreign direct investment. This rubbishes TRIPS supporters' argument that a strict patent regime increases the flow of technology and investment into developing countries.

Another topic of great importance to India is patents given to multinational companies and non-nationals on Traditional Knowledge that is held by the collective conscience in India based on its history and culture. There was an outcry and widespread criticism when American companies like W.R. Grace and Agridyne, tried to register over 50 patents related to the *Neem* tree. The bark, leaves, fruits and oil from the *Neem* tree have been used in traditional medicine in India for centuries and many in India were angry over the attempts by these companies to steal knowledge that was rightfully a collective legacy[133].

In response, India, along with other developing countries, led the efforts for a Doha Ministerial Declaration to examine the relationship between the TRIPS agreement and the Convention of Biological Diversity, the protection of traditional knowledge and folklore and other relevant issues. They submitted a framework (IP/C/W/420), to the TRIPS Council that requires patent applicants to disclose the source and country of origin of the genetic resources or traditional knowledge that are being patented. The applicants are also required to show evidence of prior consent from the country as well as evidence of benefit sharing. In 2002, India passed the Biological Diversity Act 2002, which provides for conservation of biological diversity, sustainable use of its components and fair and equitable sharing of the benefits arising from the utilization of biological resources and knowledge.

TRIMS (PART OF ANNEX 1)

The agreement on Trade Related Investment Matters (TRIMS), was the third addition during the Uruguay Round,

---

133 W.R. Grace was awarded two US patents for the extraction and storage of *Neem* extracts – US Patent No 4946681, granted in 1990, for improving the storage ability of *Neem* seed extracts containing *Azadirachtin* and US Patent No 5124349 in 1994, for storage of stable insecticidal composition comprising *Neem* seed extract. The Indian government filed a complaint with the US Patent Office accusing W.R. Grace of copying an Indian invention but later withdrew it acknowledging that a new invention in extraction and preservation had been done. (Source: Guide to the WTO and Developing countries, Peter Gallagher, 2000, Kluwer Law International and the WTO)

along with GATS and TRIPS. The TRIMS Agreement is very modest in scope today though there are efforts to enlarge it to consider agreements on Trade and Investment policy as well as Trade and Competition policy. These can significantly change the nature and scope of TRIMS and companies must keep a close watch on these developments as they can have a huge impact on the business and competitive environment around the world. As it stands today, TRIMS reaffirms existing WTO/GATT principles (such as National Treatment) and indentifies a number of trade related investment requirements imposed by member countries that are inconsistent with those principles. These measures include:

1. Local content requirement – which governments impose only on foreign players in the domestic market that requires them to source a certain percentage of the components from local suppliers
2. Trade balancing restrictions and requirements – which governments impose on foreign players which require them to maintain a certain percentage of imports with respect to their exports
3. Domestic sales requirements – which require these companies to sell a proportion of their production in the domestic market.

An illustrative list of the measures that violate the principles of GATT is annexed to the text of the agreement[134]. The agreement also requires all WTO members to notify TRIMs that are inconsistent with the provisions of the agreement and to eliminate them after the expiry of the transition period. Transition periods have been defined to be two years for developed countries, five years for developing countries and seven years for least-developed countries.

---

134 http://www.wto.org/english/docs_e/legal_e/18-trims_e.htm

India notified three TRIM related measures which were inconsistent with the provisions of the agreement:

1. Local content requirements in the production of News Print
2. Local content requirement in the production of Rifampicin and Penicillin-G and
3. Dividend balancing requirements in the case of investment in 22 categories of consumer goods[135].

There were to be eliminated by the end of 1999 and India complied with the provisions of the TRIMs agreement. India does not have any outstanding obligations under the TRIMs agreement as far as notified TRIMs are concerned[136].

TRADE POLICY REVIEW MECHANISM
(TPRM – ANNEX 3 OF THE WTO AGREEMENT)

While Annex 1 of the Marrakesh agreements covered detailed aspects of the trade agreements themselves, including the new agreements, GATS, TRIPS and TRIMs and Annex 2 covered the dispute settlement mechanism, Annex 3 established the Trade Policy Review Mechanism (TPRM) as one of WTO's basic functions, with the objective of facilitating smooth functioning of the multilateral trading system by enhancing the transparency of members' trade policies. TPRM allows for surveillance of national trade policies and WTO reviews, discusses and appraises the trade policies and practices of all its members.

A Trade Policy Review Board (TPRB), made up of the WTO General Council operating under special rules and procedures, supervises the process and submits detailed reports which are made available through the WTO

135 http://commerce.nic.in/trade/international_trade_trims_atrim.asp#b1
136 http://commerce.nic.in/trade/international_trade_trims_atrim.asp#b5

Secretariat. The Annex mandates that the four members with the largest share of world trade (US, Japan, China and the EU), be reviewed every two years; the next 16 countries be reviewed every four years; and others be reviewed every six years.

The reviews focus on the members' own trade policies and practices in the context of their developmental needs, as well as the economic environments they face. Trade policy reviews cover all aspects of country's trade policy including its domestic laws, regulations, the institutional framework, and all trade agreements with other countries. The documents published are discussed by the WTO's full membership and with other inter-governmental organizations such as the IMF/WB and UNCTAD, as observers. These peer reviews by other WTO members encourage (and goad), governments to follow the WTO rules and disciplines more closely to fulfill their commitments.

The last TPRB report on India was done in 2007. The press release on the summary of the report indicated that India needed further reforms to sustain fast economic growth (below)[137] PRESS/TPRB/283, 23 May 2007, (07-2046)/ TRADE POLICY REVIEW: INDIA/ Further reforms needed to sustain fast economic growth

India's economic performance has continued to be impressive since 2001/02 and growth has been particularly rapid since 2003/04, averaging over 8.5% with over 9% for 2006/07. This performance is largely due to unilateral trade and structural reforms, particularly in services, according to a WTO Secretariat report on the trade policies

---

137   http://docsonline.wto.org

and practices of India. Rapid economic growth has also resulted in an improvement in social indicators such as poverty and infant mortality.

The report notes that if India's high rates of economic growth are to be sustained, reforms need to be deepened – in particular to address infrastructure bottlenecks such as transport and electricity, which continue to constrain growth. In addition, further structural reforms will be required in agriculture, to address the sector's relatively low productivity and the problems faced by marginal farmers.

Continued structural reform, the report notes, together with greater investment in physical and human capital, would also help to generate much needed productive employment for new entrants to the labour force.

The report, along with a policy statement by the Government of India, was the basis for the fourth Trade Policy Review (TPR) of India by the Trade Policy Review Body of the WTO on 23 and 25 May 2007.

The following documents are available in MS Word format on the WTO web-site. They can be downloaded: http://www.wto.org/english/tratop_e/tpr_e/tp283_e.htm

Criticism of TPRM

There are two main criticisms of the Trade Policy Review Mechanism agreements:

    a. this surveillance and review of domestic policies by WTO, is a violation of the sovereignty of member countries

    b. through this mechanism, WTO promotes the

Washington Consensus of liberalization and free market policies.

In all reviews by the TPRM, policies which promote liberalization and free markets are noted as good policies by member governments, while all policies which provide domestic protection, are noted as bad policies that need to be remedied. The peer review mechanism is akin to peer pressure to conform to the liberal ideology and reviews may seem more like disciplining, directing and even warning countries to adhere to the ideology so they can be more integrated into the world economy governed by the WTO. The model country under these reviews is always the US, which the trade policy review in 1999 noted as among the most open and transparent economies in the world. Countries are encouraged and pushed to move towards the US model – the agenda of the Washington Consensus.

WTO MINISTERIAL MEETINGS & THE DOHA DEVELOPMENT ROUND

Countries (members) negotiating at the Uruguay Round, also agreed to a number of future dates for review and negotiations of specific sectors and subject areas. This is sometimes referred to as the Built-in Agenda and some of them include:

1. Reviewing Technical Barriers to Trade (TBT).
2. The Dispute settlement understanding by 1998.
3. Extension of coverage of the Government procurement agreement.
4. The appraisal of the Trade Policy Review Body by 1999.
5. Negotiations for removing agricultural protection and subsidies in 2000 among others.

The topmost body of the WTO, the Ministerial Council, is also required by the Marrakesh Agreement to meet at least once every two years to discuss matters of importance to the body. There have been eight Ministerial Conferences since WTO came into effect. At the fourth Ministerial Conference in Doha in November 2001, a new of round of trade talks was initiated, called the Doha Round — which are still ongoing as of 2011.

The first Ministerial Conference after the formation of WTO, was the Singapore Ministerial Conference in 1996. During this Conference, four working groups were set up and tasked to deal with the following issues: Transparency in Government procurement; Trade Facilitation (customs issues); Trade and Investment; and Trade and Competition. The developing countries were extremely unhappy with this Conference as the issues dealt with were primarily of importance to the developed nations and addressed none of the issues of importance to developing countries, such as reductions and elimination of agricultural subsidies in developed nations.

The second Ministerial Conference was held in Geneva, Switzerland in May 1998 and was primarily an event to celebrate 50 years of GATT. Other than plans for future negotiations and recognition of e-commerce, not much activity of significance was conducted at this Conference. The third Ministerial Conference was the Seattle Conference in 1999, which ended in complete failure. The Seattle Conference was also marred by massive protests, including violence and physical property damage by anti-globalization activists outside the State Convention and Trade Center, where the meetings were scheduled[138]. The aim to launch a new round of talks, dubbed the Millennium Round, never went beyond agenda-building. There were disagreements between the developed countries and developing countries, as well as between the US and the EU on many issues.

The location for the fourth Ministerial Conference was carefully[139] chosen as Doha, Qatar and held in November 2001. There were two main outcomes of this Conference – China was officially inducted as a member of WTO and the agenda for the next round of trade talks, known as the Doha Round, was finalized. The built-in agenda had already kicked in to start multilateral negotiations on agricultural market access and the pressure from India[140], Brazil and other developing countries, on including agricultural issues and issues of market access in developed countries in the agenda for the Doha Round of talks, set the stage for the next round of trade talks. The needs and interests of developing countries were to be the focus of the round and hence it was called the Doha Development Round. The areas identified for reform were agriculture; non-agricultural market access (NAMA); Trade in Services (GATS); developing country issues (Special and Differential treatment); and aid for trade.

The next WTO Ministerial Conference in Cancun in 2003, attempted to forge a concrete agreement on the Doha Round objectives. It ended without an agreement on a framework to guide future negotiations and this failure resulted in a serious loss of momentum. Many developing

138 Inspired by the protests, Stuart Townsend directed and released a movie called *Battle in Seattle* in 2007, depicting the protest against the WTO in 1999. The movie got mixed reviews from critics.

139 Qatar has very strict rules against demonstrations and basically guaranteed that there would be no protests against the Conference.

140 Statement by the Indian Minister of Commerce and Industry, at the Doha conference: http://commerce.nic.in/trade/st_doha_1.pdf

countries refused to consider the so called Singapore issues, unless topics of interest to them were resolved. The US-EU agricultural proposals were deemed too little and unacceptable to the developing nations. The statement by India's then Minister of Commerce and Industry, Mr. Arun Jaitley, at this Conference, reflects India's dissatisfaction with the agenda of the Doha Development Round[141]: "In our view the draft Cancún Ministerial Text is grossly inadequate on implementation issues and would severely affect the interests of developing countries in agriculture, industrial tariffs and Singapore issues. We cannot escape the conclusion that it does not accommodate the legitimate aspirations of developing countries and instead, seeks to project and advance the views of certain developed countries."

The importance India gave to reforms in agricultural trade was reflected in the same text in Section 8, which said: 'The commitment by the developed countries to eliminate distortions in world agriculture caused by their policies holds the key to resolving differences amongst us in this area. Let us also remind ourselves that the agriculture subsidies provided by the OECD countries are more than six times what they spend on official development assistance for developing countries. OECD Governments support sugar producers at the rate of US$6.4 billion annually – an amount nearly equal to all developing country exports. Subsidies to cotton growers in a developed country totaled US$3.7 Billion last year, which is three times that country's foreign aid to Africa. The net effect of subsidizing agriculture in developed countries at the expense of products of the relatively poor in developing countries is to aggravate global income inequalities.'

---

141 http://commerce.nic.in/trade/st_cancun_1.pdf

India and other developing countries, formed a new bloc of developing nations called the G20 and negotiated collectively at the WTO conference in Cancun. The G20 proposed an alternative framework to that of the EU and the US, on issues relating to agriculture at the conference and the failure of the Cancun Ministerial Meeting was viewed as a success for developing countries. The developing countries were seen as finally having the confidence to reject a deal that they viewed as unfavorable. The 6th Ministerial Meeting in Hong Kong in 2005, did not yield much result either. The deadlock on agricultural tariffs and subsidies continues and many efforts to break this have proved futile. The key players in the Doha Round – US, EU, Brazil and India – conducted bilateral or group meetings to break the impasse and after a number of meetings, the G4 summit (US, EU, Brazil and India) in 2007, collapsed in acrimony, with the developed and developing countries blaming each other for the failure.

In a speech in 2010[142], Ron Kirk, the US Trade Representative, said that the success of the Doha Round of talks depend on emerging economies like China, India and Brazil. In response, the Indian Industries Minister, Anand Sharma, has reassured that 'India is committed to the Doha Round'[143]. The Doha Round continues and eventually, if an agreement is reached, it has the potential to have a huge impact on the world for both developed and developing countries.

---

142 http://economictimes.indiatimes.com/news/economy/foreign-trade/Success-of-Doha-round-to-depend-on-India-China-Brazil-US/articleshow/5590587.cms
143 http://www.financialexpress.com/news/india-committed-to-doha-round/644468/

FINAL THOUGHTS

The world is changing rapidly. The triumvirate of (US-created) international organizations – the IMF, WB and WTO, are evolving and adapting to this changing world. As the dominance of the US is being challenged by the EU and other fast-growing, developing economies such as India, China and Brazil, its ability to control and influence the actions of these international institutions is slowly but surely diminishing. There is a slow shifting of power away from sovereign nations to international institutions that now can override many finance and trade-related domestic decisions. The developing countries have come a long way from the time when their interests were ignored to where they can now effectively derail trade negotiations if their interests are not met. They are also entering into a number Free Trade Agreements and Preferential Trade Agreements amongst themselves, integrating their economies further and creating new markets without depending on the markets in developed countries.

India has entered into a number of such agreements, including ASEAN in South East Asia, an agreement with MERCOSUR countries in Latin America and with countries in the region such as Sri Lanka, Nepal, Bhutan, Singapore and Afghanistan[144].

There is a slow but sure growing balance of power equation in the world. The stage has been set for the next evolution of the world towards a more global state and the possibility for a system of world rules that are more just. This evolution must and will continue and India has to take an active role in this process as it is slowly beginning to do. Further restructuring and empowerment of the

---

144 http://commerce.nic.in/trade/international_ta.asp?id=2&trade=i

international institutions is good not only for India but for all developing countries and ultimately for the entire world. It is time for comprehensive UN reforms and for it to be more empowered.

The Environment, Global Warming & India's Place in the Global Environmental Debate

5

Scientific consensus suggests that the earth is getting hotter, pointing to human activity as the key reason for this warming trend. In July 2010, NOAA (National Oceanic and Atmospheric Administration in the US Department of Commerce), reported that June 2010 was the warmest June on record. The combined global land and ocean average surface temperature for June 2010 was 1.22 degrees F above the 20th century average and the land surface temperature was more than 1.93 deg F above the 20th century average[145]. Normal human body temperature is 98.6 deg F and when it rises to 100 deg F, a rise of just 1.4 deg F, a doctor's visit becomes necessary and we are said to have the 'fever.' Given this standard, we can safely conclude that since the 1980s, the Earth has been struggling with a fever that is constantly getting worse[146].

The issue of global warming gained worldwide publicity with the release of *An Inconvenient Truth* by Al Gore,

145 http://www.noaanews.noaa.gov/stories2010/20100715_globalstats.html
146 http://data.giss.nasa.gov/gistemp/graphs/Fig.A2.lrg.gif

and assessment reports from the UN Intergovernmental Panel on Climate Change (IPCC), both of whom were awarded the Nobel Peace Prize in 2007.

Though global warming has caught the imagination and focus of the world, it is by no means the only environmental problem we face today. Pollution of the elements of the earth (air, water, and land), is as serious a problem and so are deforestation and the loss of bio-diversity on the planet. Rapid economic development around the world has contributed to or created a number of these problems and the most developed nations have contributed the most cumulatively to the damage of the earth's environment. The rapid industrialization of developing economies such as China, India and Brazil, threaten further damage to the already fragile environment, unless steps are taken to prevent it, including reducing energy density and creating a more sustainable growth model for the world economy.

Most predictions of future conditions on earth are dire if nothing is done to change the current course of human activity. One of the most significant international agreements to combat global warming is the Kyoto Protocol, in which more than 180 countries participated in an effort to restrict and reverse the growth of green house gases in the atmosphere. Only the US, among the major nations, is not a participant in this treaty. The Kyoto Protocol is set to expire in 2012 and the 2009 UN Climate Change Conference in Copenhagen (Copenhagen Summit), was supposed to create an agreement to replace or extend the Kyoto Protocol. But the Copenhagen Accord, drafted at the very last moment by the US and the BASIC countries of Brazil, South Africa, India and China, does not contain any binding commitment on limiting the global temperature rise; does not have a target for peaking emissions; nor any commitment to a legal treaty, leading many to dismiss it as ineffective.

The EU is the unquestioned leader in fighting global warming and has committed to implementing binding legislation even without a deal at Copenhagen. It has revised its carbon allowances system called the Emissions Trading Scheme (ETS), for the post-Kyoto period. The UN and its agencies have played a key role in the evolution of the strategy to fight global warming and pollution, as well as preserving the environment, and one of the first major UN sponsored conferences was the Biosphere Conference in Paris in 1968, sponsored by UNESCO (UN Educational Scientific and Cultural Organization).

Initial Efforts to Preserve the Environment & Combat pollution

The Biosphere Conference in 1968, was one of the first major international meetings focused on conservation of nature, the impact of human activity on the biosphere, and the need to link scientific research to the conservation of nature and natural resources[147]. This conference led to UNESCO's Man and the Biosphere (MAB) program, initiated in 1970. Under the MAB program, a global network of biosphere reserves were created in which ecological and conservation research was conducted, contributing significantly to our understanding of integrated resource management and the ways science can be used in conserving out natural environment.

---

147 http://portal.unesco.org/en/ev.php-URL_ID=30393&URL_DO=DO_TOPIC&URL_SECTION=201.html

Just as Al Gore and others have brought global warming to the forefront in the last decade, a number of writers in the 1960s, raised awareness of environmental issues and the ill effects of chemicals and pollution. Rachel Carson's book, *Silent Spring,* published in 1962, drew attention to the impact of pesticides and chemical technology on the environment. Stewart Udall published *The Quiet Crisis* in 1963, in which he wrote about the dangers of pollution, overuse of natural resources and dwindling open spaces. Udall was also instrumental in the enactment of a number of environmental laws in the US including, Clean Air; Clean Water; and Endangered Species Preservation Acts, among others. *The Limits to Growth,* published in 1972, drew attention to the growing pressure on natural resources from human activity.

Rising public concern in the 1960s, led to a number of pollution control legislations in the US, such as the Clean Air Act in 1963, later modified in 1970, and the Clean Water Act in 1972. The Clean Air Act of 1970, led to the creation of the Environmental Protection Agency (EPA) in the US. EPA is mandated to develop and enforce regulations to protect the general public from exposure to airborne contaminants that are known to be hazardous to human health. Later amendments to the Clean Air Act in 1990, added provisions for addressing acid rain, ozone depletion and toxic air pollution, as well as stabling a national permits program. The Clean Water Act was targeted at eliminating the release of high amounts of toxic substances into water so that water would meet standards necessary for human sports and recreation by 1983. On international co-operation for environmental issues, the US Congress passed the National Environmental Policy Act[148] (NEPA) in 1969, which

---

148 http://ceq.hss.doe.gov/nepa/regs/nepa/nepaeqia.htm

committed the US Government and its agencies to a policy of international co-operation in environmental affairs.

Stockholm Conference, 1972

The next major UN sponsored conference after the Biosphere Conference, was the UN Conference on the Human Environment in 1972 in Stockholm, Sweden. The objective of the conference was, 'To provide a framework for comprehensive consideration within the UN of the problems of the human environment in order to focus the attention of Governments and public opinion on the importance and urgency of this question and also to identify those aspects of it that can only, or at best, resolved through international cooperation and agreement[149]'. The Stockholm Conference had a huge impact on the world for environmental issues and legitimized environmental policy as a universal concern for all nations. For the first time, there were huge numbers of attendees from non-governmental organizations (NGOs), concerned citizens groups and other private individuals, in addition to government representatives at the conference, signifying the growing importance of environmental issues around the world. Lynton Caldwell[150] has argued that the Stockholm Conference represented a paradigm change in people's thinking about the environment, "The change marked by Stockholm is from the view of an earth unlimited in abundance and created for man's exclusive use to a concept of the earth as a domain of life or biosphere for which mankind is a temporary resident custodian."

The divergent views between the developed nations and developing nations on the topic also found expression

---

149 http://www.unep.org/Documents.Multilingual/default.asp?DocumentID=97&ArticleID=1496&l=en

150 International Environmental Policy, Third Edition, Lynton Keith Caldwell, Duke University Press, 1996

at the conference. The primary concern of most developed nations was the human impact on the environment with emphasis on pollution control and conservation of resources, while the developing nations were most concerned with social development and economic growth. The developing nations also held (and continue to hold), the view that most developed countries had caused the most damage to the environment and that they were setting restrictions on the use of natural resources in an effort to constrain the growth of developing countries. The statement made by Indira Gandhi, the then Prime Minister of India, at the Stockholm Conference, echoed the sentiments of many leaders of developing countries when she said, "Many of the advanced countries of today have reached their present affluence by their domination over other races and countries, the exploitation of their own masses and own natural resources. They got a headstart through sheer ruthlessness, undisturbed by feelings of compassion or by abstract theories of freedom, equality or justice[151]."

The conference produced a Declaration on the Human Environment[152], an Action Plan for the Human Environment, and a Resolution on Institutional and Financial Agreements. The Declaration contained 26 principles concerning the environment and development – of which, Principle 21 has played in important role in the evolution of international environmental diplomacy and agreements. It states, 'States have, in accordance with the Charter of the United Nations and the principles of international law, the sovereign right to exploit their own resources pursuant to their own environmental policies, and the responsibility to

---

151 Ibid 120
152 http://www.unep.org/Documents.Multilingual/Default.asp?DocumentID=97&ArticleID=1503&l=en

ensure that activities within their jurisdiction or control do not cause damage to the environment of other States or of areas beyond the limits of national jurisdiction.'

The Action Plan contained 109 recommendations for six broad issues: human settlements; natural resource management; pollution of international significance; education; and social aspects of the environment development and environment; and international organizations. This last set of recommendations led to the creation of the UN Environmental Program (UNEP).

UNEP

The U.N. General Assembly recognizing the urgent need for a 'permanent institutional arrangement within the United Nations system for the protection and improvement of the environment', adopted resolution 2997, which led to creation of the UNEP (United Nations Environmental Program), with its headquarters in Nairobi, Kenya (one of the few UN body headquarters located outside the EU and US, with the developing countries playing a major role in its creation, as well as its location). The UNEP has a Governing Council of 58 States elected by the General Assembly and an Executive Director, also elected by the General Assembly. The UNEP Secretariat was to be small and serve as a focal point for environment-related activities within the UN.

The main objectives for UNEP were laid out in the text of Resolution 2997[153], and are primarily to coordinate, catalyze and inform the UN General Assembly on the state of the world's environment as well as possible policy guidance to deal with the issues. The UNEP has a very small budget of $30 Million and a staff strength of around 200 personnel.

---

153 http://www.un-documents.net/a27r2997.htm

Despite the enormous size and complex nature of the issue, as well as a role that is primarily to influence, without any authority, and a limited budget and personnel, UNEP has managed to play a significant role in the development of many treaties and agreements that have helped formulate an action plan against global warming and the protection of the environment.

One of UNEP and the UN's greatest successes in facilitating a multilateral environmental agreement is the Montreal Protocol. The Montreal Protocol, to phase out ozone depleting chemicals in the upper atmosphere, has been hailed by many including Kofi Annan, as one of the most successful international environmental agreements negotiated under the UN. UNEP also helped organize the UN Conference on Environment and Development in Rio de Janeiro, Brazil – also called the Earth Summit, where the Framework Convention on Climate Change (UNFCCC), was negotiated and a formal treaty signed. The Kyoto Protocol, an international agreement to limit the amount of green house gases (GHG) in the atmosphere, is a culmination of efforts under the UN Framework Convention on Climate Change. UNEP, along with the World Meteorological Organization, established the Intergovernmental Panel on Climate Change (IPCC[154]). in 1988, which has been very influential in conducting research and publishing documents related to global warming.

These assessment reports highlight the possible changes to the environment (rise in global temperatures, climate disruptions, coastal flooding, desertification etc), if the emissions of green house gases (GHG) are not checked.

154 The Chair of the IPCC is Rajendra K Pachauri, an Indian, who along with Al Gore received the Nobel Peace Prize on behalf of the IPCC

IPCC was awarded the Nobel Peace Prize along with Al Gore in 2007, for its path-breaking work.

The Montreal Protocol

In the 1970s, scientists in the US (Paul Crutzen, Mario Molina and Frank Rowland[155]), showed that (Chloro-Fluoro-Carbons – primarily used in refrigeration and aerosol applications), CFCs, released into the atmosphere, were the primary cause of a growing 'ozone hole' in the ozone layer of the atmosphere. Ozone absorbs most of the harmful radiations from the sun, protecting us from their harmful effects, including skin cancer. Its depletion presented a real threat. In 1985, a British Antarctic survey revealed a large ozone hole over the Antarctic – far larger than anyone had expected. This rallied international attention to the problem, leading most major CFC producers to sign the Vienna Convention, which established a framework for negotiating international regulations on ozone-depleting substances.

Negotiations began under this framework in Montreal and in September 1987, the Montreal Protocol was signed by 24 nations, providing for a gradual phase down of CFC production and consumption by industrialized countries to 50% of their 1986 levels, by 1998-99, with a 10-year grace period for developing nations. India and China opposed this treaty, citing both lack of financial and technical resources to comply with the provisions of the agreement. Maneka Gandhi, India's then Minister for the Environment in 1989-1991, argued that, "The industrial nations created the problem in the first place so they should pay for cleaning it up[156]".

---

155 They were awarded the 1995 Nobel Prize for Chemistry, for their contribution to the understanding of the depletion of the ozone layer.
156 http://www.entrepreneur.com/tradejournals/article/9334063.html

At the subsequent conference of parties in London 1990, a number of the concerns raised by India were addressed, including the setting up of a Multi-lateral Fund[157] for financial support as well as pledges for transfer of technologies to developing countries and other concessions such as extended grace periods, were negotiated and incorporated into the agreement. India acceded to the protocol along with the London amendments in 1992. The Ministry of Environment and Forests in India set up an ozone cell for co-ordinating the implementing the Montreal Protocol, as well as function as the nodal agency for requesting grants under the Multilateral Fund[158]. India has continued to maintain this stand of differentiated responsibilities for developed nations and developing nations – which was also incorporated in the UN Framework Convention on Climate Change (UNFCCC).

The Montreal Protocol has since been amended at Copenhagen and Vienna, and the number of controlled substances has been increased from the original eight to over 80 by 1995[159]. Since the Montreal Protocol came into effect, the atmospheric concentrations of CFC have stabilized or decreased but it has led to another problem – Hydro-Chloro-Fluoro Carbon (HCFC) and Hydro-Fluoro Carbon (HFC), chemicals which were used to replace CFCs, are now thought to contribute to global warming.

---

157 http://www.multilateralfund.org/
158 A list of the projects supported by the multilateral fund can be found at: http://cpcbenvis.nic.in/newsletter/ozone-sep-1994/sept94ix.htm.
159 http://www.eoearth.org/article/Montreal_Protocol_on_Substances_that_ Deplete_the_Ozone_Layer

THE EARTH SUMMIT

The UN Conference on Environment and Development (Earth Summit), was held in Rio de Janeiro in 1992, a full 20 years after the Stockholm Conference in 1972. The Earth Summit was one of the largest UN sponsored conferences ever, with more than 170 governments participating and over 27,000 people attending, as well as a parallel NGO forum called Global Forum. The goal was to get governments to rethink economic development without the destruction of irreplaceable natural resources and pollution and to create policies and decisions that took into account their effect on the environment. Agenda 21[160], a wide-ranging blueprint for action to achieve sustainable development, was adopted at the conference. It contained detailed proposals for action in social and economic areas such as combating poverty, changing patterns of production and consumption and addressing demographic dynamics. For the first time, sustainable development became the centerpiece of the discussion and debate and led to the creation of the UN Commission on Sustainable Development.

The Earth Summit was also the venue where the Convention on Biological Diversity (CBD) was opened for signatures. Article 1 of the CBD text defines the objectives as: 'The objectives of this convention, to be pursued in accordance with its relevant provisions, are the conservation of biological diversity, the sustainable use of its components and the fair and equitable sharing of the benefits arising out of the utilization of genetic resources, including by appropriate access to genetic resources and by appropriate transfer of relevant technologies, taking into account all rights over those resources and to technologies, and by

---

160 http://www.un.org/esa/dsd/agenda21/

appropriate funding[161]'. The US did not sign the treaty – in part to protect its pharmaceutical industry. It is not part of the Convention of Biological Diversity, a stance it has taken in many international environmental agreements, including the Kyoto Protocol. Kamal Nath, the then Indian Minister of Environment and Forests, led the Indian delegation at the Earth Summit. His tirade against the US for not signing the Convention on Biological Diversity[162] and his efforts on the Framework Convention on Climate Change, made him one of the chief spokesmen for the developing countries.

The Earth Summit was also where the UN Framework Convention on Climate Change (UNFCCC), was ratified by the attendees as a response to fight global warming. The aim of the convention was to stabilize greenhouse gas concentrations in the atmosphere at a level that will prevent dangerous and irreversible damage to the global environment. The Framework itself provided guidelines and was non-binding, but placed the heaviest burden for fighting climate change on industrialized nations, as they were the source of most of the accumulated green house gases in the atmosphere. The developed nations were listed in the first annex to the treaty and are called 'Annex 1 countries' – and were expected to reduce their levels of emission in 2000 to those levels in 1990 (that is the economic growth between 1990 and 2000 must be at no extra GHG emissions). Annex 1 countries also agreed under the convention to support climate change activities in developing countries by providing technical and financial support.

----

161 http://www.cbd.int/convention/articles.shtml?a=cbd-01
162 http://www.nytimes.com/1992/06/12/world/earth-summit-delegates-4-nations-warm-high-profile-role-global-powerbroker.html

Since the UNFCCC came into force, the parties to the agreement have met annually in Conference of the Parties (COP), to negotiate more binding agreements for GHG reductions, as well as to assess progress in dealing with climate change. The first Conference of Parties (COP) took place in 1995, in Berlin, and established a two-year Analytical and Assessment phase to create the structure and options for a more binding mandate. The second meeting (COP 2), took place in 1996 in Geneva — which highlighted emerging differences between the US and other countries. The third meeting or COP 3, took place in 1997 in Kyoto, Japan. For the first time ever, members came together and agreed on a protocol (Kyoto Protocol), that set binding greenhouse gas emissions reductions for Annex1 countries along with flexible mechanisms that allowed developing countries to participate — such as the clean development mechanism and the joint implementation mechanism.

The Kyoto Protocol

The Kyoto Protocol was adopted on 11 December 1997, and was enforced on 16 February 2005. Under the Kyoto Protocol, emissions for six main greenhouse gases (Carbon Dioxide, Methane, Nitrous Oxide, Hydroflurocarbons, Perfluorocarbons and Sulphur Hexafluoride), were targeted for reduction. As agreed under the UNFCCC, the Kyoto Protocol placed the burden of the reduction for these gases on the developed nations. On an average, a 5% reduction against 1990 levels[163] of the gases, was targeted by the end of 2012. The EU undertook the highest level of reduction of these gases at 8% by 2010, while the US was given the task of reducing emission by 7% against 1990 levels. Canada, Hungary, Japan and Poland agreed to a 6% reduction, while

---

163 http://unfccc.int/kyoto_protocol/items/2830.php

New Zealand, Russia and Ukraine agreed to a 5% cut[164]. The US never ratified the Kyoto Protocol and is not a party to it. Successive US Presidents have argued that the targets would hurt domestic industry and were generally in favor of smaller targets[165]. The detailed rules for the implementation of the Protocol were adopted at COP 7 in Marrakesh in 2001, and are called the Marrakesh Accords.

Under the treaty, Annex 1 countries must meet their targets primarily through national measures, through the protocol offers them additional means of meeting their targets by way of three market-based mechanisms: emissions trading; clean development mechanism; and joint implementation.

Emissions trading is a market-based approach to achieve the required reductions in GHGs, committed to by Annex 1 countries. EU countries calculate and set a cap on the total emissions in their country and allocate emissions permits (the right to emit a specific amount of gas), to different firms. Firms are required to hold equivalent permits (or credits), for their emissions – and those that need to increase their emissions, buy additional permits from those who need or use fewer permits. Some companies invest in clean technologies to reduce their emissions and have extra credits that they can sell to other companies who are inefficient. In this way, inefficient producers pay for the extra pollution they create and those that reduce their emissions are rewarded. The largest market is the EU Emission Trading Scheme and is the EUs central policy to meet their cap set in the Kyoto Protocol.

---

164 http://unfccc.int/kyoto_protocol/items/3145.php
165 The world seems to be bypassing the US when it comes to environmental agreements and is an area where the US has not been able to use its economic or military might to influence other countries.

The Clean Development Mechanism allows developing countries to participate in reducing GHGs by allowing them to sell credits they can generate by undertaking projects that reduce the emission of GHGs above and beyond what would be considered normal or baseline. Examples include solar rural electrification. The normal or baseline for developing countries would be electricity generated in a coal fired power plant. By installing a solar electric system, the government can contribute to a reduction in baseline emissions. Once this is calculated and certified, the government has credits or CERs (Certified Emission Reduction), that it can sell on the global market as carbon credits. This creates financial incentives for developing nations to invest in clean technologies and grow their economies with lower energy intensity.

The primary growth of GHGs in the coming decades is going to come from fast growing developing countries such as India and China. As these countries begin to invest in infrastructure, specifically the energy infrastructure, there is now an incentive to invest in renewable energy infrastructure which otherwise would be too expensive, as compared to coal-based power plants, which are one of the main sources of GHGs in the atmosphere. The CDM mechanism has been operational since 2006, and has so far already registered more than 2650 projects, for a total estimated reduction of more than 2.9 billion tones of CO2[166]. China and India are by far the largest generators of CERs, combining for more than 60% of the total CERs created in non-Annex 1 countries[167]. India also has among the lowest CO2 emissions per capita, as well as one of the lowest

---

166 http://unfccc.int/kyoto_protocol/mechanisms/clean_development_mechanism/items/2718.php
167 http://cdm.unfccc.int/Issuance/cers_iss.html

energy intensity economies in the world[168].

Joint Implementation is the last of the flexibility mechanisms under the Kyoto Protocol and allows Annex 1 countries to invest in emission reduction projects in the so called economies in transition, noted in Annex B of the Protocol. Russia and Ukraine host the greatest number of JI projects, with Russia alone accounting for almost two-thirds of the projected emission reductions.

India ratified the Kyoto Protocol in 2002, and since then, has been an active participant through the CDM mechanism[169]. The Kyoto Protocol went into effect in 2005, and 141 countries have ratified the Protocol, including every major industrialized country except the US[170]. There has been a lot of debate about the status of India and China as Annex 2 countries, without binding limits on reductions in their emissions, as China is now the world's largest emitter of GHGs and with a rapidly growing economy, India's emissions too, are on the rise. Many have also argued that the commitments in the Kyoto Protocol are too small to make a real impact on the problem[171]. The first phase of the Kyoto Protocol ends in 2012, and negotiations for the second phase or another agreement were targeted for the Copenhagen Summit in 2009.

---

168 http://siteresources.worldbank.org/INTWDR2010/Resources/5287678-1226014527953/Statistical-Annex.pdf
169 http://www.rediff.com/news/2002/aug/28earth1.htm
170 A number of businesses in the US including Oil, Car and other companies opposing the Kyoto Protocol citing damage to their businesses and have lobbied successfully preventing the US from ratifying the protocol
171 Scientists have recommended a reduction in the range of 35-40% in GHG emissions from the base set in 1980

Copenhagen Summit

The UN Climate Change Conference in Copenhagen, opened on 7th December 2009, with much fanfare and a lot of expectations for a binding agreement that would significantly cut GHG emissions and limit global warming. The EU continued its global leadership in addressing the global warming challenge by committing to binding legislation even without a satisfactory deal in Copenhagen and revised its Emissions Trading Scheme for the post-Kyoto period. It also committed to cutting emissions unconditionally by 20% from 1990 levels by 2020, and proposed to cut emissions by 30% if other big emitters take tough action. The EU advocates for rich nations to make an 80-95% cut by 2050, to slow emissions growth.

In contrast, negotiations between the US and the developing countries brought the discussions to a complete standstill. The US insisted on targets for developing countries to slow the growth of emissions and for international scrutiny of domestic emissions reduction actions taken by developing countries, while opposing legal commitments and obligations such as those under the Kyoto Protocol. The US also proposed a cut in emissions of only 17% below 2005 levels by 2020, which is a mere 4% below 1990 levels, which pales in comparison to the required reduction in the order of 35-40% below 1990 levels.

The developing countries led by China and India, wanted the developed countries to make substantial binding reductions in the order of 35-40% below the 1990 levels, funding and technology transfer to developing nations to cut emissions, and non-binding reductions in energy intensity without committing to a peaking year[172]. They were also opposed to international scrutiny of domestic efforts at emission reductions, but were open to scrutiny of projects funded by international capital[173].

India's main argument continues to be to put the blame for climate change on the developed nations and for discussions based on per capita emissions as opposed to total emissions as an idea of carbon equality. China was ready to set a binding goal to cut CO2 per unit of GDP by 40-45% below 2005 levels by 2020, but wanted the developed countries to cut emissions by 40% below the 1990 level and pay 1% of their GDP every year to help other countries adapt[174]. India was willing to cut CO2 emissions per unit of GDP by 20-25% from its 2005 levels but rejected a legally binding target[175].

The US, led by President Barack Obama, reached a deal with China, India, Brazil and South Africa, on the last day of the Conference and tabled the Copenhagen Accord in the final session. It was taken note of but not adopted in a debate of all the participating countries. The accord is not legally binding and does not commit countries to agree to a binding successor to the Kyoto Protocol. Many countries and NGOs were opposed to this agreement and

---

172 A peaking year is the year theoretically when a country's emissions peak after which the emissions start reducing. India and China are opposed to committing to a peaking year as they focus on economic development to lift millions of their citizens from poverty and cannot commit to a specific year. Also committing to a peaking year will keep their per capita emissions substantially lower than in developed countries.

173 http://news.bbc.co.uk/2/hi/science/nature/8345343.stm

174 Ibid 143

175 http://www.thaindian.com/newsportal/world-news/india-china-versus-united-states-at-copenhagen_100291027.html, http://www.hindu.com/2009/12/04/stories/2009120456550100.htm

there were many critics to the backdoor policy-making by the US and the BASIC countries. The main opposition came from the ALBA bloc of Latin American countries. Venezuelan delegate Claudia Salerno Caldera, said the deal was a "coup d'état against the authority of the United Nations[176]". Environmental campaigners and aid agencies branded the deal toothless and a failure.

The key points of the Copenhagen accord are[177]:

- It is not a legally binding agreement and neither is there a deadline to transform it into one. The Accord was merely recognized by the 193 nations at the summit. It is not clear if it is a formal UN deal.
- The text recognized the need to limit global temperatures rising no more than 2C above pre-industrial levels, but is not a formal target. The Accord also does not identify a year by which carbon emissions should peak.
- The deal promises to deliver $30 Billion aid to developing nations over the next three years and a goal of providing $100 Billion a year by 2020, to cope with the impacts of climate change. The fund will support projects in developing countries related to mitigation, adaptation, capacity building and technology transfer.
- Pledges by rich countries will come under rigorous and transparent scrutiny under the UNFCCC, while developing countries will submit national reports on their emission pledges under a method that will ensure their sovereignty is respected.
- The implementation of the Accord will be reviewed by 2015.

The UN Secretary General Ban Ki Moon, welcomed the climate deal as an, "essential beginning", but wanted it made legally binding.

---

176 http://news.bbc.co.uk/2/hi/science/nature/8422133.stm
177 http://news.bbc.co.uk/2/hi/science/nature/8422307.stm

Many research reports have outlined the possible impact of global warming around the world and most agree that they affect different regions in markedly different ways. "Ironically, the places that have contributed the least to greenhouse gases and those least able to cope will be the most affected," says Jonathan Patz, a professor at UW-Madison[178]. Coastlines along the Pacific and Indian oceans and sub-Saharan Africa, will bear the brunt of the effects of global warming. India is one of the most vulnerable countries and many coastal cities such as Kolkata, will be badly affected. Global warming will affect agricultural productivity and water availability which will disproportionately impact the more than 400 Million people that make up India's poor.

The Indian government launched a comprehensive scientific program to assess the impact of global warming under the Indian Network on Comprehensive Climate Change Assessment (INCAA), bringing together 125 research institutions around India. The Indian government also launched an ambitious solar energy initiative to generate 22,000 megawatts of electricity from solar power by 2022 and in a first among major economies, India introduced a Carbon Tax of 50 rupees per ton of coal used, to fund clean energy research and development[179]. This tax will help build India's National Clean Energy Fund and jump-start the renewable energy industry, including the ambitious solar electricity plan. Such efforts demonstrate India's commitment to reducing the energy intensity of its economy and in fighting global warming. But it must also continue to work on creating a more binding agreement at the international level. India has also updated a number

---

178 http://news.mongabay.com/2005/1118-wisc.html
179 http://www.justmeans.com/In-India-a-New-Carbon-Tax-Will-Fund-Renewable-Energy/21298.html

of its environmental laws to comply with international standards and agreements.

India's Environmental Laws[180]

India enacted the Water (Prevention and Control of Pollution) Act in 1974, and later amended it in 1988[181] - to provide for the prevention and control of water pollution and to maintain or restore the wholesomeness of water in the country. In 1981, the Air (Prevention and Control of Pollution) Act was enacted and later amended in 1987, to provide for the prevention, control and abatement of air pollution in India[182]. The Central Pollution Control Board is the chief central agency with the responsibility of enforcing these laws.

The Environment (Protection) Act was enacted in 1986, with the objective of providing for the protection and improvement of the environment and preventing environmental pollution in all its forms. In 2000, a draft of the ozone depleting substances regulation rules, was published to control the production and emission of such substances – incorporating agreements from the Montreal protocol. A National Environment Appellate Authority (NEAA), was set up by the Ministry of Environment and Forests, to address environmental clearances for certain restricted areas under the National Environment Appellate Authority Act of 1997. A new National Green Tribunal Bill 2009, is pending in Parliament, which will pave the way for setting up a National Green Tribunal to settle civil disputes concerning environment-related issues.

---

180 http://moef.nic.in/modules/rules-and-regulations/ifs/
181 http://moef.nic.in/modules/rules-and-regulations/water-pollution/
182 http://moef.nic.in/modules/rules-and-regulations/air-pollution/

The Wild Life (Protection) Act 1972, was amended in 2003. Punishment and penalty for offences under the act have been made more stringent. There is a draft amendment bill 2010, which will fully implement India's international obligations under the International Trade in Endangered Species of Wild Fauna and Flora (CITES) Convention which India became a party to in 1976. This amendment will establish a Management Authority to regulate trade in exotic species of animals and plants that are alien to India.

The Biological Diversity Act 2002, aimed at the conservation of biological resources and associated knowledge, as well as facilitating access to them in a sustainable manner, was based on the UN Convention on Biological Diversity held in 1992. The Act established the National Biodiversity Authority in Chennai, to implement the Act.

FINAL THOUGHTS

Global warming represents one of the most critical environmental problems facing the world and only a concerted international effort (with legally binding agreements), can help mitigate its effects. The EU continues to be a leader in this effort, while most other countries have not shown enough commitment to tackle the issue. India also faces the additional problems of pollution of its natural resources due to the rapid (environmentally poorly regulated) growth of its economy. The outcome of the Copenhagen Summit is not encouraging for the world's poor, who will be most affected by global warming. India, along with the G20 and others, must do more to help control greenhouse emissions and mitigate the efforts of global warming.

India is also slowly making progress in a number of areas including new legislation to tackle pollution, protect its bio-diversity and natural resources. New efforts such as the Carbon Tax and the ambitious Solar Mission, provide hope for the future. A consequence of growing awareness of environmental issues, increasing local and international regulations and global trade treaties, will be the upward harmonization of the regulatory environment for businesses. Businesses will continue to face growing regulations on energy usage, GHG emissions, pollution treatment and other environmental requirements and must be proactive and prepared to not only deal with them but to build strategies that will give them a competitive edge over their rivals. Strategic investments into energy efficiency, renewable energy and pollution treatment and emission reduction technologies, can help them differentiate themselves in their industry.

Afterword

India is integrating itself with the world again and at an accelerating pace since the economic reforms and liberalization process that started in 1991. India is playing a meaningful role in discussions and agreements at the WTO and on environmental issues. India's strong foreign currency reserves and a fast growing economy, have helped it turn from a borrower into a contributor of funds at the IMF. India wants a greater say in the collective security arrangement of the UNSC and is campaigning for a permanent seat at the Security Council. While world power has not shifted East, there is a growing sense that the developing countries have become a force to reckon with. There are calls for reforms and restructuring of the major international institutions, reflecting this slow but sure shift towards a new global balance of power.

India's place in the world can be viewed through four different aspects that govern international relations today: Security, Finance, Trade, and the Environment. India needs to make strategic choices for all these aspects in order to grow on the international stage. A strong military with the will to project power and use it, will enhance India's place in the world of security. A careful monetary liberalization policy, along with policies that attract foreign investment, will enhance India's place in the world of finance. Leveraging India's natural advantage in the services industry and enabling the movement of people, along with further opening up of the economy, will enhance India's place in the world of trade. Leading the fight against climate change with a strong focus on the technologies of the future such as renewable energies and pollution control technologies geared for low income countries (a Tata Nano version of pollution control devices and technologies), will enhance India's place in the environmental world.

As the world gets more integrated through trade, many regulatory regimes in developing countries will be harmonized to catch up with the regimes of the developed countries. This shift in regulation poses both risks and opportunities for businesses in developing nations. If they are not prepared for the changes, they will vanish, replaced by more strategic and forward thinking companies that embrace this change and make strategic choices in anticipation of the changing regulations. Companies in India and other developing countries, must review their corporate strategies to incorporate the changes brought about by globalization and integration.

The four aspects for companies to evaluate are: political and security risks; financial risks, including currency fluctuations and devaluation; trade barriers; and changing regulations for environmental protection. Companies investing abroad must evaluate the political and security risks in the countries they invest in – to protect physical property as well as their personnel. Availability of political risk insurance, either through governmental agencies or the World Bank, should be used to hedge against it. Financial instability poses many risks, including changing costs of doing business, difficulty in raising money and exchange rate fluctuations. These risks should be constantly evaluated and hedged against in the market. Companies must be aware of trade policies, tariff and non-tariff barriers to trade and the changing agreements being negotiated under the WTO, as well as the global standards for their products. Finally, companies must anticipate coming environmental regulations and incorporate them into their strategies to give them an edge in the market.

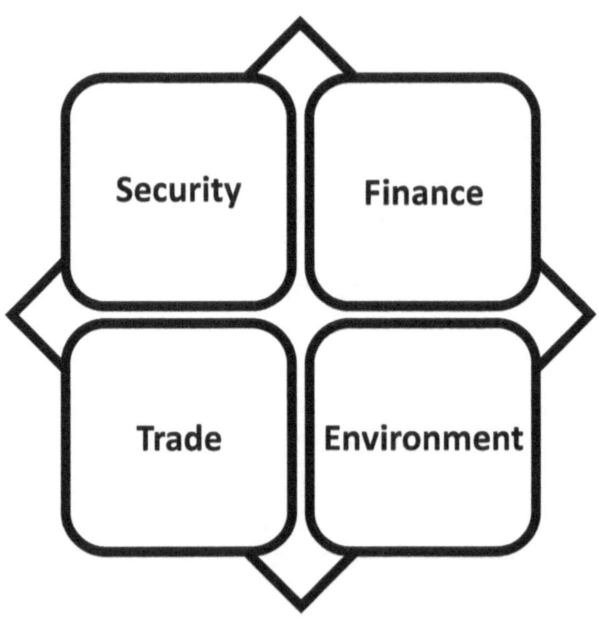

Four essential aspects of a global strategy

ACKNOWLEDGEMENTS

I would like to particularly thank Professor Roy Nelson at the Thunderbird School of Global Management, for inspiring me with his lectures on the 'Global Political Economy'. The idea for the book, as well as large portions of it, have been based on his lectures – though I have adapted them to my interest in India's role in the world and viewed the content through 'Indian eyes'.

I would also like to thank my colleagues and friends at Thunderbird, whose company, thoughtful criticisms and discussions on the subject, helped me refine the material as well as stay positive during the writing of the book. My special thanks goes to Anurag Gupta and Balaji Govindan. The library at Thunderbird has been an invaluable resource in the writing of this book and I extend special thanks to the staff for their support and help.

I am grateful to Chandralekha Maitra and the team at Leadstart Publishing, for believing in the manuscript and publishing the book. They have been a delight to work with. I also extend my sincere thanks to Rhonda Lee Carver, who helped me edit the book and make it a lot more readable.

My family has been an incredible source of support and encouragement and I would not have been able to write the book without their love and support. I owe them immense gratitude. I hope my boys Arya and Roanakh, grow up to live in a world that is more fair and just and where all countries work together to solve critical issues such as global warming.

SELECT BIBLIOGRAPHY

Barnett, Michael & Finnmore, Martha. *Rules for the world: International Organizations in Global Politics*, Cornell University Press, 2004

Brown, Chris. *Understanding International Relations*, St. Martin's Press, 1997

Caldwell, K Lynton. *International Environmental Policy*, Duke University Press, 1996

Correa, M. Carlos. *Intellectual Property Rights, the WTO and Developing Countries*, Zed Books Ltd. 2000

Foreign Services Institute, India. *India's Foreign Policy*, Academic Foundation, 2007

Freeman, Jr. Chas. *Arts of Power, Statecraft and Diplomacy*, United States Institute of Peace Press, Washington DC, 1997.

Gallagher, Peter. *Guide to the WTO and Developing Countries*, Kluwer Law International, 2000

Gilbert, L. Christopher & Vines, David. *The World Bank, Structure and Policies*, Cambridge University Press, 2000

Goddard, C. Roe. Passe'-smith, John & Conklin, John. *International Political Economy*, Lynne Rienner Publishers, 1996

Guzzini, Stefano. *Realism in International relations and International Political Economy*, Routledge, 1998

Jackson, H. John. *Restructuring the GATT System*, Royal Institute of International Affairs, 1990

Jackson, H. John. *The World Trading System*, MIT Press, 1998

Hoekman, Bernand. Mattoo, Aaditya & English, Philip. *Development, Trade and the WTO*, the World Bank, 2002

Khanna, Parag. *The Second World*, Random House, 2008.

Mahbubani, Kishore. *The New Asian Hemisphere – The Irresistible shift of Global Power to the East*, Public Affairs-New York.2008.

Mohanty, Bijoyini & Hazary, S.C. *Political Economy of India*, A.P.H Publishing Corporation, 1997

Nayar, Baldev Raj and Paul, T.V. *India in the World Order*, Cambridge University Press, 2003

Nehru, Jawaharlal. *Independence and after: a collection of speeches 1946-1949*, Published in the US by The John Day Company, 1950, 1971.

Purfield, Catriona & Schiff, Jerald *India goes global*, International Monetary Fund, 2006

Riggs, E. Robert & Plano, C. Jack *The United Nations*, Wadsworth, 1994

The World Bank, *A guide to the World Bank*, 2007

Thirkell-White, Ben. *The IMF and the Politics of Financial Globalization*, Palgrave Macmillan, 2005

Toussanint, Eric. *The World Bank – A Critical Primer*, Pluto Press, 2008

Vines, David and Gilbert & L. Christopher. *The IMF and its Critics*, Cambridge University Press, 2004

Vreeland, R James. *The International Monetary Fund – Politics of Conditional Lending*, Routledge Global Institutions, Routledge, 2007

Yoder, Amos. *The Evolution of the United Nations System*, Taylor and Francis, 1993.

www.ingramcontent.com/pod-product-compliance
Lightning Source LLC
Chambersburg PA
CBHW051252250726
48656CB00004B/1246